Making Sense *of*
Martin Luther

Making Sense *of* Martin Luther

David J. Lose

AUGSBURG FORTRESS

Minneapolis

MAKING SENSE OF MARTIN LUTHER

Scripture quotations, unless otherwise marked, are from New Revised Standard Version Bible, copyright © 1989 Division of Christian Education of the National Council of Churches of Christ in the United States of America. Used by permission. All rights reserved.

References to LW are from Martin Luther, *Luther's Works*, American edition, ed. Helmut Lehmann and Jaroslav Pelikan, 55 vols. Philadelphia: Fortress Press/St. Louis: Concordia Publishing House, 1955–1986.

ISBN: 978-1-4514-2555-0

Cover design: Joe Vaughan
Interior design: Ivy Palmer Skrade
Typesetting: Tory Herman
Illustrations: Jean Sinclair

The paper used in this publication meets the minimum requirements of American National Standard for Information Sciences—Permanence of Paper for Printed Library Materials, ANSI Z329.48-1984.

Manufactured in the U.S.A.

24   23   22   21   20   19   18   17   1   2   3   4   5   6   7   8   9   10

Contents

Dedication

To the staff and campers at Mount Olivet Lutheran Church's Cathedral of the Pines Camp—a new generation of Christians committed to living in and sharing the freedom of the gospel—and to those who preceded them and through their vision, faith, and generosity made COP possible.

Acknowledgments

This was an unexpected book in the sense that it was not part of the original series of *Making Sense* books I had planned to write. Given the 500th anniversary of the Reformation occurring this year, however, it made good sense to use the conversational style of writing that had been helpful in explaining topics like how to read scripture and the meaning of the cross in order to open up Martin Luther's theology for a new generation of Christians.

Even though it "made good sense," this book would not have come to completion were it not for the help of several colleagues. Beth Lewis, Tim Blevins, and Martin Seltz at 1517 Media approved an accelerated timeline to get this in print for the fall of 2017. Laurie Hanson, editor for this volume, reviewed chapters with remarkable speed, insight, and grace. Scott Tunseth, editor of previous volumes, was among those who offered helpful feedback that much improved the book.

Two of my teachers and colleagues stand behind much of my own understanding of Luther. Timothy Wengert, emeritus Ministerium of Pennsylvania professor of Reformation history at the Lutheran Theological Seminary at Philadelphia, introduced me to the theology of Martin Luther in a way that captivated me in my first year at seminary and continues to stretch and challenge me to apply Luther's thought to our daily lives all these years later. The late Gerhard Forde, Tim's teacher and my colleague for several years at Luther Seminary, shaped my thinking through his very accessible writing, particularly *Where God Meets Man: Luther's Down-to-Earth Approach to the Gospel* (Augsburg Books, 1972); the influence of his concept of "up-and-down religion" will be evident in these pages.

This book came together during a period of significant and creative transition, both professionally and personally. Professionally, I worked on this manuscript while helping to unify the Lutheran Theological Seminary at Philadelphia and the Lutheran Theological Seminary at Gettysburg, two historic institutions that had separated more than one hundred and fifty years earlier. I want to thank my colleague president at Gettysburg, Michael Cooper-White, and the boards at both schools for their vision and courage, and to express my gratitude to the students, staff, and alumni of these seminaries for their support of this endeavor. Personally, I lived this past year apart from my family as they moved back to the Twin Cities while I stayed in Philadelphia to complete the consolidation. I'm grateful to my wife, Karin, and children, Katie and Jack, for their love and support during a turbulent time.

Finally, I am grateful both to and for the people of Mount Olivet Lutheran Church—a vibrant congregation in Minneapolis and Victoria, Minnesota—who called me to be their senior pastor and were willing to wait nearly a year for me to finish work on unifying the two Pennsylvania seminaries before I could join them. I am grateful for their faith, patience, and trust, and I am regularly inspired by their commitment to share in word and deed the "faith of our fathers"—and mothers!—with a new generation of Christians.

As I mentioned earlier, I wrote this book in light of the 500th anniversary of the start of the Reformation. To be perfectly honest, however, I am more interested in the 600th anniversary and, quite truthfully, the question of whether there will be a 600th anniversary. With so many demands on their time and a plethora of other significant narratives available to them, the emerging generation will not simply go to church because their parents did, but will only invest themselves in something they see as meaningful and worthwhile. Consider this book, therefore, as one small gesture toward introducing Luther's dynamic understanding of God's life-changing gospel to a new generation, with the hope that they find it as interesting, useful, and ultimately captivating as did their parents.

Introduction

Luther as Monk, Myth, and Messenger

Over the past five hundred years, Martin
Luther has received numerous accolades and been credited with shaping some
of the most important intellectual movements and societal views that endure
to this day. In a lecture in 1835, Ralph Waldo Emerson said, "Martin Luther
the Reformer is one of the most extraordinary persons in history and has left
a deeper impression of his presence in the modern world than any other except
Columbus."[1] More than a century and a half later, Luther came in third—behind
Columbus and Thomas Edison—in *Life* magazine's list of the 100 most influential people of the millennium.[2] Variously heralded as the founder of the Western
notion of individual conscience, advocate of the separation of church and state
enshrined in the U.S. Constitution, promoter of religious equality and freedom,
and champion of God's justifying grace, his mark on world history is undeniable.

But Luther's legacy is by no means entirely admirable. His polemical writings against the Jewish people of his day were used by the Nazis to justify their
abominable actions. Some believe his words calling for violence against protesting peasants sparked oppression that killed tens of thousands of people.

Good or bad, loved or hated, Luther achieved nearly mythic status even
before he died. This only grew in the years and centuries to come. Yet despite all
this attention, few people know all that much about Luther and, more importantly—at least to Luther—his theology. Oh, they know he was a monk, he nailed

1

ninety-five theses to a church door and ignited the Reformation, and he founded a church that took his name as its own. And, if pressed, some may know he believed in justification by faith (though they might not understand what that means) or remember his famous words, "Here I stand," when facing down the emperor of his day.

Much of this "common knowledge," however, is increasingly debated. Historians have questioned whether Luther swung a hammer or used beeswax to affix his theses to the door of the Castle Church in Wittenberg. (Beeswax was more common, but not nearly as dramatic!) His sermon series on his *Ninety-Five Theses*, rather than the theses themselves, probably had greater influence in popularizing his reforms. Luther was aghast at the notion that Christians would take his name rather than the name of their Lord and Savior. And there is some doubt whether he uttered the statement "Here I stand" or—as with other sayings attributed to him—this was the creation of later myth.

Fortunately for us, we don't need to resolve these matters. Rather than spend time on the details of his life, Luther would want us to grapple with the substance of his theology—that is, his way of making sense of how people experience God in their lives and the world. He would want us to focus on theological convictions like God's justification of sinners by grace through faith, the role of scripture as norm of norms in all matters of faith, the first and second uses of the law, the primacy of the gospel, the two hands or governments of God, God's call to each and all of us to care for our neighbor and the world in whatever roles we may play, the surprising nature of God being revealed to us in love where we least expect God to be, the importance of the grace freely given through the sacraments, and our simultaneous condition of being both fully justified and fully sinful.

What Luther would want most, however, is for us to meet the same God he met in and through his study of scripture. He would want us to know the same assurance, even confidence, that we are beloved by God, promised our salvation purely and entirely by grace, and used by God for the ongoing care of the world. He would want us to see in Jesus' life, death, and resurrection the absolute promise that God comes to us in love, eager to grant to us Christ's own righteousness. In other words, more than a monk, and far more than a mythic figure, Luther comes to us five hundred years later as a messenger. In one of the most famous pieces of artwork seeking to capture the heart of the Reformation, Luther stands in a pulpit to the right side of the painting, a crowd of people on the left, pointing to a figure of Christ on the cross. That's Luther—in everything he did he wanted people to see Christ and particularly to see God's love for the world revealed in Christ's crucifixion.

Portion of altarpiece at St. Mary's Church, Wittenberg, by Lucas Cranach the Elder (1472–1553).

This book seeks to draw you into Luther's theology in a way that makes it both understandable and useful. *Understandable* to help you imagine and make sense of what was at stake for the great reformer in various elements of his theology. *Useful* in the sense that Luther's theology is not merely a historical or even theological matter but is practical—informing our day-to-day faith and life. Throughout the book, I present what I have found most useful in my own life of faith. This means I've made some choices—I don't cover everything I find interesting about Luther in these seven chapters. It also means you'll get my biases. Not all will agree with which elements of Luther's theology I chose to lift up, or even with how I present them, but if those disagreements spark further conversation, one of the aims of this book will have been met.

I have chosen to write in the form of a conversation between two persons. One voice knows a little more and assumes the role of teacher or coach, someone who has had the time and opportunity to study the faith in some depth. The other voice assumes the role of the student or novice, someone who is curious and knows a little bit about the faith but brings a lot of questions. It may be tempting to imagine the first voice is the more important of the two, but I want to suggest the second voice is equally and in some ways perhaps more important, as the questions asked and insights offered are finally what move the dialogue forward.

I chose this way of writing—which may take a little getting used to—because I have found time and again that I learn best in and through conversation. And I don't think I'm alone, as there's something about the give-and-take of conversation that helps to stretch us. If we can imagine the brain metaphorically as a muscle, then conversation is one of the most effective ways to exercise and strengthen that muscle. As you read the book, I hope that hearing some of your own questions embodied in the voice of the earnest, honest seeker gives you confidence to start your own conversations with others about Luther and ultimately about your faith. (And should you want to write down some of your own questions and insights, there's always a place to do so at the end of each chapter. Go ahead, it's your book!)

While I've used this conversational format in the other Making Sense books and materials published by Augsburg Fortress, it seems particularly appropriate when treating Martin Luther. Dialogue, written out or spoken in "live time," was a beloved tradition in the Reformation. Indeed, Luther's *Ninety-Five Theses* were written precisely to spark a dialogue on the use of indulgences in the church. They were not offered or received initially as a radical protest but as an invitation to scholarly conversation and debate.

The dialogue in this book begins with a chapter on Luther's context and then dives into the central theological impulse of the Reformation—that we are justified freely by grace through faith. It moves forward with the various implications of this single insight as it relates to our experience of God (law and gospel), God's continuing influence in our lives (two kingdoms), our life as Christians called to care for the world (vocation), and God's surprising presence in Jesus' cross and the sacraments. It concludes with a discussion of Luther's painful—and, at places, simply awful—writings about his Jewish neighbors, using these to look at both the limitations and continued vitality and importance of Luther's theology.

I have said on occasion that Luther helps me remain a Christian. Here's what I mean by that. In contrast to many religious thinkers and writers, Luther is remarkably down-to-earth and committed to a realistic view of the life of faith. His theology does not take you away from the world, let alone rescue you from its challenges, but rather immerses you in the world convinced that God is there— in the world and our lives—already at work and eager to meet us in grace and to use us for the good of our neighbor and world.

I hope these reflections help you make sense of Luther's theology and, more importantly, help you make sense of your life of faith in, with, and under the grace of the God we know most fully in and through Jesus the Christ.

CHAPTER 1

The Reluctant Reformer

*Introducing "the Monk
Who Changed the World"*

So, I'd like to ask you some questions about Martin Luther.

Sure. Go ahead.

Some of them might be dumb.

There is no dumb question.

Everyone says that.

Maybe. But I mean it. Actually, I think *not* asking your questions is kind of dumb. Because if you don't ask, how are you going to learn?

Okay. But you're sure it's all right?

Absolutely, why wouldn't it be?

I don't know. I guess I feel like I should know more about Luther. After all, I grew up in a Lutheran church.

But you don't go to one now?

Oh, I still do. And that makes it worse. I mean, I don't go all the time, but I go enough to feel like I ought to know more about the guy our church is all about.

Actually, maybe that's the first thing I can tell you about Luther.

What?

That he'd be a little bummed out to hear someone say the church is all about him.

Why? I mean, it's got his name and everything.

True, but that wasn't Luther's idea. In fact, when he first heard folks call themselves "Lutherans," he got kind of mad.

Seriously?

Oh, yeah. He said he was nothing more than a "bag of maggots"[1] and that he cringed at the thought that the children of God would take his name.

Okay, I have to agree with you. It does sound like he was both mad and bummed out that people called themselves Lutheran. But I'm still not sure why.

Because Luther saw himself first and foremost as a follower, not a leader.

A follower?

Yes, he identified first and foremost as a follower of Jesus. He didn't set out to lead anything or to attract followers.

But didn't he start the Reformation? I mean, wasn't he the leader of that whole thing?

Maybe, but not on purpose.

Why not?

Because Luther wasn't trying to start anything. He was simply trying to be a decent pastor to his people.

Say more.

Prior to the start of the Reformation, Luther is a monk who's serving as a professor at a relatively new university in a little German town called Wittenberg. In addition to teaching classes on the Bible, part of his job is to hear the confessions of people in the town.

Hear confessions?

Yeah, confession was part of the practice of faith at the time . . . and it still is for many Roman Catholic Christians today. In Luther's day, before you could go to church and receive communion, you had to confess your sins. The priest would give you something to do, called *penance*, to help you acknowledge your mistakes and put you back on the right track. Then you could go to church and take communion and have your sins forgiven.

And this was important?

Very. The church at that time was concerned about forgiveness, sin, and hell. So an elaborate system was developed and administered by the church to help you avoid the consequences of sin and receive forgiveness so you could go to heaven.

A "system" of sin and forgiveness?

Yeah. As I said, it was pretty elaborate and highly organized, and confession and penance were important elements of it. Part of Luther's job as a monk is to hear people confess their sins so he can give them penance and they can go to communion. But after he's been doing this for a while, he begins to notice that his people seem less and less interested in actually coming to confession.

But I thought you said it was important.

Exactly. Really important. Which makes Luther curious. And when he starts asking around, he finds out that people don't feel they need confession all that much because they've bought indulgences.

What's an indulgence?

Essentially, an official document of the church that said you were forgiven a certain amount of sin.

Kind of like a "get out of jail free" card, but for hell?

More or less. Instead of confessing your sins and doing penance, you bought an indulgence.

Doesn't sound like a bad deal, at least if you had the money.

Maybe, but to Luther it pretty much undercuts the whole idea of confession.

What do you mean?

Confession wasn't only about naming your sin, doing penance, and going to communion. It was also about repentance.

And how is repentance different from penance?

Penance was something you did to make up for something you'd done wrong. Repentance, though, is more about going back out into life determined to do things differently, to do them right. The word used in the Bible for *repentance* actually means to turn around, to go another way.

Interesting. And so that's what was missing. The turning around and living differently.

Right. Luther believes indulgences are not at all like going to confession, but more like an official permission slip to sin.

Like in James Bond?

What?

You know, in the movies. James Bond had a license to kill, and indulgences gave people a license to sin.

Pretty much. Not that the church intended it that way, but it ended up being the way indulgences were used. If some folks got drunk some evening, for instance, instead of coming to confession the next day, doing penance, and trying to change their lives . . .

They could just pull out their indulgences and go get drunk again.

Right. And that makes Luther really mad.

He seems to get mad a lot.

He does, and that's something we'll eventually come back to. In this case, Luther feels indulgences are not only undermining confession but also ruining people's lives because they feel they have permission to be their worst selves, to never try to get any better or improve their lives. Even worse, at least for Luther, indulgences seem to take something that's supposed to be free—God's love and forgiveness—and sell it to make money for the church.

So, what does Luther do?

He starts investigating and finds out the situation is even worse than he'd thought.

How so?

Well, it turns out that people aren't only buying indulgences for themselves. They're also buying them for their relatives.

I guess that makes sense. Kind of like a medieval gift card.

And not only for their living relatives, but for their dead ones too.

Whoa—hold on! I don't think gift cards are supposed to work like that. Why in the world would you buy an indulgence for someone who's already dead? I mean, it's not like they could use it.

Actually, they could. You see, people believed that indulgences didn't just buy forgiveness of sins in the present, but also forgiveness—of anyone's sins—from the past or into the future. Which meant that buying an indulgence for someone who had already died could cut down their time in purgatory.

Sorry, you lost me. I was following you until you got to purgatory. What's that?

It's kind of like a waiting room.

Come again?

Well, this will take some explaining and take us back to what we mentioned earlier about the church's system of sin and forgiveness and all the rest.

No problem. I've got time.

Okay, so I said earlier that sin and forgiveness were pretty much everything in Luther's world.

I remember.

But it might be more accurate to say that sin was really at the center of things, and that everything else helped you deal with it.

Say more.

The church of the Middle Ages taught that humans were sinful through and through.

Cheery.

You have no idea. Essentially, according to the church at the time, people were sinful down to the core, and right from birth.

From birth?

Yeah. The idea was that "the fall"—when Adam and Eve sinned—tainted all of humanity and the result was what's called "original sin." And all humans ever since Adam and Eve have this original sin and therefore stand under God's judgment and deserve to go to hell.

Hold on. Just because Adam and Eve screwed up, everyone ever since deserves God's punishment? That doesn't seem fair. Did Luther believe this? I mean, Adam and Eve, the fall, original sin, heaven, hell, all the rest?

This was the world Luther grew up in. It was a very different world from ours, in terms of how people imagined the universe working. There wasn't much science to speak of, at least as we know it today. And it was a world animated by angels and devils, where the possibility of ending up in either heaven or hell was a pretty constant concern. Some of Luther's thinking on all this changed, matured over time. But at this point, this was his world.

Okay, so I understand a little more about how sin is at the center of everything. But say more about the system that helped you deal with it.

Sure. Because of original sin, humans are born into what was called a state of sin. And that was not just bad, but downright dangerous, because if you died in a state of sin, you would go to hell. And so the church had this comprehensive system to keep you out of a state of sin and put you in a state of grace. And the first part of that system was baptism.

What we do with babies?

Exactly. You brought your baby to the church to be baptized and that, more or less, granted forgiveness for original sin.

Well, I still don't think it's fair that babies were considered sinful when they hadn't done anything yet, but at least baptism took care of that. What came next?

Even though your original sin was forgiven, for the rest of your life, every time you sinned you fell out of a state of grace and back into a state of sin.

Which is bad, because if you died in a state of sin you were doomed.

Right. And that's where the whole sacramental system came in.

"Sacramental system"?

Yes. Seven sacraments were used to help people get out of a state of sin and into a state of grace so they could go to heaven.

Okay, I may not know a whole lot about Luther, but I know that we don't have seven sacraments. We only have two, right?

In the Lutheran church and in other churches that come from the Reformation, yes. But in the Roman Catholic Church of the time— and in the Roman Catholic Church today—there are seven sacraments. Baptism and communion . . .

Those are the two I know.

Confession and penance, like we talked about, are a third. Then there's confirmation, anointing of the sick, ordination, and marriage.

Wow. You weren't kidding when you said this whole thing was comprehensive and complex.

Definitely. But it all worked together in an amazingly organized way. And confession and penance were so important . . .

Because they allowed you to move back to a state of grace.

Right, and prepared you for communion, which also granted forgiveness and gave you access to the treasury of merits.

The what?

Like I said, this is a bit complex. Maybe the easiest way to think of all this is to compare it to banking.

Banking?

Yes, or more specifically, the system of credits and debits that banks work with.

Okay, I do my banking online and never took an accounting class, so could you explain this a bit more?

No problem. Whether you bank online or in person, everything about your bank revolves around credits and debits. Every time you put money in the bank, you're credited with having that amount. And every time you pay a bill online or use your ATM card to take out cash, that amount is a debit and is subtracted from your account.

Straightforward enough.

The medieval church thought about things in a similar way. Every time you did something good, something God wanted you to do, you racked up credits, and every time you did something bad . . .

You got some debits. I get it.

Right. Except that you began with an enormous debit.

Original sin.

Right again.

Which I still think is totally unfair.

I know. But that's how they looked at things. And original sin created a problem. You started out totally in the hole, in a state of sin, and there was no way a baby could do anything good to get some credits in his or her account and wipe out the debits.

And that's where baptism came in?

Yes. According to the medieval church, in baptism God forgives our original sin and starts us out with an even balance.

That explains why baptism is so important, but what about the other six sacraments?

They come into play because no one lives a sinless life. So even though you're forgiven for original sin, every time you mess up you fall back into a state of sin and need some way to make it up.

And that's what the other sacraments do? Baptism takes care of original sin, and the rest of the sacraments help you out with all the other sins?

Right. Each time you sin you get some debits, so you need to do good things to get some credits to even things out again. But we often can't do enough good things—they were sometimes called "good works"—to even out all the bad things we do, so we need access to some other credits.

Wait, I'm getting confused. Can we go over this part again?

Sure. Imagine it this way. You've racked up a whole lot of debits . . .

Hey, sorry, but can I interrupt for a second?

Sure.

Okay, so all this talk about debits—did they really think humans were so bad? I mean, did people back then go around robbing or killing each other all the time? I know the Middle Ages were tough, but were people so awful that all they had were debits?

I see what you mean. No, the world may have been rougher than it is now, but the people weren't all that much better or worse than we are today. The problem was that you didn't get debits only for really awful things. You got them any time you sinned. And essentially any time you didn't do what God wanted you to do, you sinned. Whether you insulted someone, forgot to pray, had bad thoughts about someone, and so on—all of these, as well as what we think of as more major sins, counted as debits.

Wow. When you put it that way, I probably rack up hundreds of debits a day. So how did anyone ever get out of the hole?

That's exactly the point. You couldn't, at least not on your own. Which is where the treasury of merits came in. That was the place that stored up all the excess merits of the really, really good people—the people the church called saints. They did more good works than they needed, so they had credits left over.

And all those went into the treasury of merits.

Right, and those merits—or what we've been calling credits—were added to Jesus' merits, and that's why there were enough merits for everyone else.

What do you mean, "Jesus' merits"?

Well, earlier we said everyone sins and gets debits. But Jesus was sinless, so he didn't have any debits. More than that, he spent his whole life healing and helping people, so he piled up tons of credits. And then he died on the cross for us when he didn't have to, and that created what they called a "superabundance" of merits—more merits than anyone would ever need.

So Jesus made the first massive deposit in the bank they called the treasury of merits.

More or less.

Okay, this is beginning to make sense. We start out in the hole, but baptism wipes the slate clean. Every time we sin, even the littlest bit, we rack up debits. While we can earn credits by doing good works, most of us don't earn nearly enough, but we can get hold of the merits of Jesus and the saints by using the sacraments and, I guess, by buying indulgences.

Right.

But how do purgatory and indulgences for dead people fit into all this?

Essentially, no matter how many credits you earn or buy, odds are it's not enough to get you into heaven. We just do too many things wrong. We should all go to hell, but God doesn't want to send us to hell, so the system of sin and forgiveness stretches from the sacraments of this world to purgatory in the next.

Sorry, I'm still not totally with you.

Okay, let's stick with the banking imagery for a little longer. As recently as a couple centuries ago, in some places, if you racked up so much debt that you couldn't pay it off, even after they took your house and belongings and everything else, they'd send you to what was called "debtors' prison" to work off everything you owed.

And purgatory's like that?

Right. Purgatory is the place where you hang out and wait until you've done your time, worked off all your debits, so you can go to heaven.

Doesn't sound too fun.

No, but it beats going straight to hell. At least this way you'd eventually make it to heaven.

And how long could it take?

Centuries.

Seriously?

Seriously. And that's where the indulgences come in. They allow you to buy some years off the time your friend or relative is spending in purgatory.

I'm guessing they were pretty popular then.

Yes. Which is why Luther is upset. One of his fundamental convictions is that God forgives sin freely, and he feels that indulgences undermine this.

So the church at the time didn't believe God forgave sin?

Here I want to be both careful and clear. The medieval Roman Catholic Church absolutely believed God was gracious and forgave sin. The eventual difference between Luther and the church was about our *access* to that grace and forgiveness. The medieval church focused on human works—some action or activity or practice that gave you access to God's grace and mercy. And that's essentially what indulgences were—something you could *do* to access grace.

I see.

Moreover, and from the perspective of a parish pastor, Luther observes that this creates absolutely no motivation for leading a better life, which is what he believed God wanted all along. I mean, the point of forgiveness isn't so you can go out and sin some more, but rather so you have the chance to change and live the kind of abundant life God wants for all people.

So it sounds like he didn't buy into the sacramental system.

Actually, quite the contrary: early in his career, he totally buys into it.

What do you mean? I thought you just said he thought indulgences were a bad thing.

Definitely, but indulgences weren't part of the sacramental system originally. They were introduced much later.

Why were they introduced then?

To raise money.

To raise money? You're kidding me! You mean, like a fundraiser?

Pretty much. Actually, they didn't start out that way. One of the first times indulgences were used was to raise an army. Pope Urban II wanted to go and fight Turkish Muslims living in the Holy Land, so in 1095 he granted a complete indulgence for all the sins of anyone who went and fought in his crusade. By the time of Luther, however, indulgences were used for all kinds of causes, and regularly to raise money for building projects. In fact, the indulgences sold to Luther's people were raising money to build St. Peter's Basilica in Rome.

Interesting. I had absolutely no idea. So Luther doesn't object to the sacramental system as a whole, he objects to indulgences.

Right. He soon starts questioning more and more elements of the whole system, but it's the indulgences that initially really bother him.

Well, I have to say I'm with him on this. I mean, the whole indulgence thing is beginning to sound crass.

You have no idea. Folks would go from town to town selling indulgences like door-to-door salespeople. A guy by the name of Johann Tetzel even used a jingle to help him in marketing indulgences: "As soon as the coin in the coffer rings, the soul from purgatory springs."

Yikes. Not just crass but creepy.

Right, and Luther feels this is the ultimate violation, as God's grace has become nothing more than a fundraiser. So indulgences are doing harm both to the people who buy them, by never inviting true repentance, and to God, by undermining the central affirmation of the Bible that God loves and forgives us freely.

And this is when Luther starts the Reformation?

Believe it or not, he has no intention or desire to challenge the church or start a reformation. In fact, when he protests the sale of indulgences, he actually thinks he's doing the church a favor.

Really?

Yeah. Luther is convinced that the pope, the head of the Roman Catholic Church, probably doesn't have any idea what's going on and will be appalled to find out. Luther figures that by protesting the sale of indulgences, he's helping the pope.

Kind of like a medieval whistleblower?

Exactly.

Which means he isn't trying to pick a fight?

Not in the least.

And he is a loyal Roman Catholic?

More than loyal, he is devout. At the start of his career, Luther has no particular problems with the sacraments, or with doing good works, or even with doing other things to earn credits. He has a few questions, but for the most part he buys into the system lock, stock, and barrel. For instance, Luther himself once walked to Rome on a business trip for his group of monks.

Wait, he was on foot? That had to be close to a thousand miles!

Pretty much, and across the Swiss Alps . . . during winter. But that's what you did back then. Once Luther gets to Rome, he's thrilled at the opportunities to earn all kinds of spiritual rewards. He walks up the steps of one of the more famous churches, saying prayers on each step, hoping to get his grandfather out of purgatory. And he's confident this will work. Interestingly, he begins to wonder about how effective and faithful all this is, even as he reaches the top of the steps. But at this point these are nagging questions, not anything near a change of heart, and he's pretty committed to working the system—in the best sense of that phrase—as much as he can.

No kidding! I have to say that he sounds like a pretty intense guy.

Definitely. In fact, it's precisely because he is both devout and intense that he ends up shaking things up.

Say more.

Well, as we said, at the beginning Luther completely endorses the sacramental system and treasury of merits. He just doesn't like the way indulgences end up selling God's grace. But along the way, he's so committed to the system of sin and forgiveness that he gets a bit obsessive about his own sin and isn't convinced he can ever earn enough merits to make up for it.

What do you mean?

Well, let's back up a bit. To understand Luther's theology, or his beliefs about God, it might help to know a little about Luther's background and the context in which he grew up.

Sounds good.

So, Luther is born into a family experiencing what today we would call "upward mobility." His father is a miner, and he's done well enough to hope that Luther will do even better.

Like the "American dream" where every child does better than their parents?

Right—except in a medieval, German kind of way—but that's essentially it. Luther's parents do well enough to send him to college, and their hope is for him to become a lawyer, a major step up.

Sounds like a plan. But it obviously doesn't work, or we wouldn't have churches named after Luther. Or did they name churches after lawyers back then?

No, you're right. Things don't go quite according to plan. In fact, they go—at least from the point of view of Luther's dad—horribly awry.

Why?

Because of a thunderstorm. Well, at least that's what some people say.

Now you've lost me.

Luther goes to a college at Erfurt, a town in central Germany, and starts law school there as well. It's about fifty miles from where he grew up, in Mansfeld. As the story goes, early in his career as a law school student, while traveling from his home back to school in Erfurt, he's caught in a ferocious thunderstorm with torrential rain, lots of lightning, wind, and all the rest. Luther is terrified—so terrified, in fact, that he cries out to St. Anne for help.

St. Anne?

According to church tradition, St. Anne is the mother of Mary and the grandmother of Jesus. More importantly for Luther, though, she's the patron saint of miners and protector of those caught in storms.

Sounds like a good choice then. You know, you mentioned earlier that the people who were really good were called saints. But just how many saints were there?

Tons. And with their extra good works, the saints not only contribute some of their credits to the treasury of merits, but it was believed that they were also in a position to help people still struggling on earth.

Got it. So, Luther cries out to St. Anne for help.

Right. And he vows that if she helps him, he will become a monk.

Why a monk? Why not just a really good lawyer who helps people who are in trouble or something like that?

Great question. In Luther's day, there was a feeling that there was a variety of spiritual classes.

Hmm. You're going to need to slow down here.

Okay, so you know how today we talk about a lower class, a middle class, and an upper class?

Sure.

Well, it's kind of the same in this case, except it isn't a monetary or economic system of classes, it's a spiritual one. Everyone has a chance to lead a good life and earn credits. But some jobs or ways of life put you in an upper spiritual class. They are by definition holier and therefore what you aspire to if you are more devout.

And so monks are higher than lawyers.

Yeah. It's not quite that specific, in terms of particular jobs. It's more like there is regular work—miners, lawyers, teachers, farmers, and the rest—and then there is spiritual work—priests, bishops, monks.

Okay, I've got it. So to show his devotion, or maybe just to motivate Anne to save him, Luther promises to jump up a class and become a monk.

Exactly.

And after the thunderstorm, instead of thinking maybe this was something panic induced, he feels he needs to keep his promise?

Yeah. Again, Luther is both pretty intense and devout, as we've seen, and he considers this a vow made to God.

Okay, but his decision doesn't exactly go along with what his family is hoping. How do they react?

They are mad, really mad. His dad can hardly talk to him for a while.

But eventually they come around?

Parents usually do. So once Luther changes his studies and becomes a monk, his parents reconcile with him and come to the church service when Luther celebrates his first mass.

Mass? That's like communion.

Yes, and the church stresses that in communion the priest changes ordinary bread and wine into the actual body and blood of Jesus.

Wait. The priest changes ordinary bread into Jesus' body and the wine into Jesus' blood?

That's the idea. It's called "transubstantiation" and is something we'll get back to. For now, though, it's enough to know that the family gets over their disappointment and supports Luther in becoming a monk, and they show that by coming to the service where he's going to perform the mass for the first time. It's a really big deal because only priests can do it.

Nice. Sounds like it's a good day for the Luther family.

Actually, not so much.

Why, what happens?

Well, this gets back to the whole devout-and-intense thing about Luther. Luther takes the whole sacramental system so seriously that he can't believe he has actually been invited to change bread into Jesus' body. I mean, he feels that this act—which, keep in mind, creates the possibility of forgiveness for all the people present—is so incredibly holy and important that it should be way above him.

So he feels inadequate?

Totally, completely, absolutely inadequate. He essentially has a panic attack and just can't pull it off. He retreats more or less in failure.

Poor guy! What happens after that?

Eventually, he gets up the courage to celebrate the mass, become a monk, and continue his studies. He's assigned to teach at a relatively new university in the town of Wittenberg.

Which is where he helps out with things like confession.

Right, and preaching too.

And this is where Luther runs into the issue about indulgences. Got it. But that raises another question for me.

Shoot.

Since indulgences are bringing in cash for various church-related building projects, I'm guessing Luther's protests aren't very popular.

That's right.

But he keeps it up.

He has a way of not giving up on things.

Because he takes everything so seriously?

Right. As we've already seen, he's intense. But just to be clear, Luther's intensity goes way, way beyond what most of us think of as intense. It seems like an incredible religious devotion that knows no bounds. One example of this is his terror at celebrating the mass. Another example is his obsession with sin. Particularly his own.

How do you mean?

Part of a monk's life is to go to confession regularly, but Luther doesn't just go from time to time. He usually goes every day. And he doesn't just go every day. He spends hours in the confessional.

Hours? How much trouble can you get into in a monastery?

Not that much. At least that's what his confessor thinks.

"Confessor"?

That's the person who listens to your confession and then gives you penance to do. Luther's confessor, a guy named Johann—or John—von Staupitz, is kind of a mentor and spiritual advisor to him. And von Staupitz thinks Luther is taking his own sin way too seriously. You see, Luther tries to remember every bad thing he's done. Every unkind thing he's said. Anything he should have done and didn't. Anything he thinks wasn't perfectly pure or holy.

My word! I see what you mean. No wonder he spends so much time in the confessional.

Too much time. In fact, von Staupitz eventually tells him not to come back until he has sinned enough to have something interesting to confess! Yet when Luther is done confessing everything he can think of, he goes away worried that he's forgotten something.

I think that goes beyond intense and devout to obsessive.

Maybe. You wouldn't be the first to think so. But keep in mind how high the stakes are. In Luther's world, heaven and hell are, quite literally, always hanging in the balance. Then he becomes a monk and feels it's even more important that he gets it right. This same kind of intensity colors everything about his early years. Because he doesn't just become a monk, he joins an Observant Augustinian order.

"Order"?

Think of it like a chapter of the Lion's Club or even a franchise of some larger organization. There were different orders of monks— Augustinians, Franciscans, Dominicans, and so on.

Got it.

And the Observant Augustinians were known for how seriously they took the monastic life. Once a monk, Luther works incredibly hard at being the best monk he can be, praying more, working more, trying to do as many good deeds as he possibly can, trying to do whatever penance is assigned and then some.

Sounds like he wants to go to the monastic Olympics.

That's a pretty good description. Not so much in a competitive sense, as in trying to beat everyone else at the monastery, but Luther thinks of himself as a "spiritual athlete," someone training to be as righteous as possible.

How does that work out for him? I mean, if he's spending hours in the confessional, even after making a pilgrimage to Rome, it doesn't sound like he's all that confident about his progress.

No, he continues to feel not only inadequate but increasingly like he can never measure up.

So what does he do?

Well, this is where his confessor, von Staupitz, comes in. He's something of a mystic.

A mystic? Like a wizard?

Not quite. A mystic is someone who believes that the most effective path to relationship with God isn't simply through doing good works—or even confessing your sins—but rather through humility, essentially emptying yourself and dissolving into God.

"Dissolving into God"? Sounds rather mysterious.

Hence the name.

Ah. Okay, but how does it work?

Think of it this way, if the traditional path is assertive, and in this sense positive—doing all the things you are supposed to do—the mystical path is more negative. Not negative in the sense of being a downer or overly critical. But negative in the sense of *negating* things. Letting go of yourself, not getting hung up with all the usual things people worry about—money, power, family, status—and in this sense removing all the barriers between you and God.

So the mystical path is about saying "no" to all the things in life that might distract you from God. That's what you mean by a "negative path"?

Right. Get rid of all the stuff that keeps you from God and then, in all humility, dissolve, or melt, into God's person and presence so you can feel God's love for you.

Interesting. It actually reminds me of what a Buddhist friend of mine talks about trying to do through meditation.

There are definite similarities. But in Luther's case, it just doesn't work.

How come?

Well, he ends up treating it like it's still a goal to reach, and he just can't. He can't empty himself. He can't become humble enough to experience God mystically. At least that's what he feels.

I have to say I find that confusing. I mean, given all his time in the confessional, not to mention his feelings of inadequacy, he sounds pretty humble, not at all overconfident.

But that's the problem. The minute someone like Luther feels he's making progress in being humble, he takes that as a sign of pride and has to start all over again.

Sort of a Catch-22.

Right. And that's the way Luther feels about most of his life at this point. Like he's trapped. The harder he tries to be holy, the more he knows he isn't. The more he confesses, the more he can think of to confess the next time. And the more humble he tries to be, the more proud he feels about his attempts to be humble!

Sounds awful.

It is. There's a German word Luther uses to describe the immense tension and stress he feels: *Anfechtung*.

Doesn't sound pleasant. I'm guessing it isn't quite the same as Fahrvergnügen in the old Volkswagen ad campaign.

Not at all. It essentially means "the anguish of the soul." Later in life, in fact, Luther would look back on this period as about the worst time of his life. He feels totally and completely stuck.

So how does he find a way out?

He doesn't.

But . . .

A way out finds him.

Say more.

In the middle of all these struggles, Luther is still doing the primary thing he was called to Wittenberg University to do: teach the Bible. And while he's reading and studying and teaching the scriptures, he has an insight that changes everything.

And what is that?

That it isn't up to him.

What do you mean?

That it isn't his job to be righteous, holy, and pure.

Whose job is it?

It's God's job.

I'm not sure I follow.

Luther realizes there is no way he can either make himself righteous on his own or earn God's forgiveness. Only God can do those things, so he should stop trying.

That's sounds like the negative path you talked about earlier. Stop trying and *do*. Isn't that essentially what von Staupitz told him?

I think it was actually Yoda who said that. But seriously, even on the path to mysticism, Luther feels he's still trying to *do* something, even if it's trying to let go and negate himself. Here, he realizes it isn't about trying or even doing, it's more about realizing what God has *already* done. And what God has done is to send Jesus into the world to make real God's promise to love us, accept us, and regard us as righteous and holy no matter what.

But you said Luther is mad at the people selling indulgences precisely because once you have an indulgence, you don't have to do anything, you don't have to change your life.

Yes, but there's a subtle and important difference. With an indulgence, God isn't all that involved. At best, God passively sits back, waiting for you to buy your way out of purgatory. From then on, you don't have to do a thing, because you've kind of paid your fine in advance. But what Luther realizes is that God isn't passive, God isn't sitting back waiting for you to become holy or make yourself righteous. And God is definitely not hanging back waiting for you to buy an indulgence. Rather, God is busy, constantly at work for the good of God's people. And one of God's favorite ways of working for our welfare is in forgiving and blessing people like Luther—and like you and me! And once you realize that, you can get busy too. But now your busyness doesn't need to be about making God happy. Instead, it's about loving your neighbor and making a difference in the world.

That's a lot to take in.

Yeah, Luther thinks so too. In fact, he spends the rest of his life trying to live into this one single, critical, life-changing insight: Righteousness, grace, forgiveness—these aren't things you earn or achieve but can only receive as a gift.

So the church at the time didn't believe that?

It's important to know that the church of Luther's day also believed God was gracious and forgiving but felt that our access to this grace was through our own efforts, which made the promise of God's grace conditional. In contrast, Luther feels that simply recognizing what God has done for us in Christ is enough. By building this elaborate system of merits and indulgences and all the rest, the church had set itself up as the middleman between God and God's people. And that's what Luther objects to most. For him, simply accepting God's forgiveness in faith is enough.

That sounds pretty good. I'm still not sure I get it all yet, but I like the way it sounds.

That's understandable. Like I said, it takes a while to sink in for Luther too, and so we can certainly come back to this later. For now, though, it's enough to recognize that two important things come out of this time in Luther's life that guide most of what he does from this time forth.

"Drum roll please . . ."

The first is the conviction that God loves the world and takes the initiative to redeem people. This insight becomes the center of what will later be called the Protestant Reformation. The second is that this kind of knowledge isn't available to us by reason but only by revelation.

Hmm. Say more about the second one.

Luther feels that reason—our ability to think things through—is a God-given gift and is incredibly useful in understanding the creation. But it also has its limits. It can't figure everything out. And one of the things it can't figure out is God, because God is not a part of creation but instead is the creator. Nature can give you clues but not a clear picture. Only those things God has revealed in scripture can give you true knowledge of God. So while Luther may have stumbled upon his insight about God's love, he stumbles on it while reading scripture. That is, he doesn't figure it out himself; he finds it by reading and studying God's revelation in the Bible.

Why is this important?

Because it becomes the basis of Luther's authority to challenge, well, pretty much everyone, from the local religious magistrates, to the regional bishops and cardinals, and eventually the pope himself. Luther places the authority of scripture above all else when it comes to theology. Eventually, one of the rallying cries of the Reformation becomes *sola scriptura*, Latin for "scripture alone."

I'm guessing the pope doesn't like this.

An early reformer, Jan Hus, had been burned at the stake for saying that the pope was not the final authority on all matters. And so, no, the pope doesn't like it. In fact, Luther is excommunicated.

Which means . . . ?

Technically, it means you're no longer allowed to receive communion and, in effect, are thrown out of the church.

Which is pretty bad, since it's the church and communion that give you a chance to receive forgiveness.

Exactly.

What does Luther do?

By this time, he's becoming convinced that the church is in the trouble it's in precisely because it hasn't been following what scripture says, but instead has been following what mere humans—that is, popes and cardinals—are saying. So Luther holds a party and burns the paper sent to him about his excommunication.

Feisty!

And then some. But only because of his convictions that, first, God is the one who saves us and, second, that all authority ultimately rests on scripture. But that doesn't mean he ever quite gets over his insecurity or doubt.

What do you mean?

Well, for example, once Luther's theological reforms begin to take hold, he's summoned to a diet to answer for himself.

A "diet"? Like something you do to lose weight?

Actually, it's a kind of conference dedicated to making rules and settling disagreements. In this case, it's held in a German town called Worms, so Luther is summoned to the Diet of Worms.

"Diet of Worms." That doesn't sound appetizing.

I know, it doesn't come off too well in English, but in Germany at the time it was a big deal, running for several months to discuss all kinds of imperial business. Sort of like a session of Congress. And at that meeting, presided over by the emperor himself, Luther is confronted with a pile of his own books and other writings and asked two questions. First, does he recognize these books as ones he wrote? And, second, is he prepared to stand by everything he wrote or is he willing to recant, that is, admit he was wrong?

Pretty dramatic! What does he do?

He answers the first question in the affirmative, saying he recognizes his works. And he asks for another day to think about the second question. And when they come back the next day, Luther says that he can't recant because he trusts scripture more than he trusts church councils or even the pope. He finishes by saying, "My conscience is captive to the Word of God. I cannot and I will not retract anything, since it is neither safe nor right to go against conscience. I cannot do otherwise, here I stand, may God help me, Amen."[2] And that, many say, is essentially the start of the Protestant Reformation.

HOLY BIBLE

Here I stand!

Even though Luther doesn't imagine going down this path?

That's where that word "captive" is so interesting. Luther isn't looking for a fight. He's not looking to change the world, and throughout
his life he's plagued by bouts of insecurity. But he can't seem to help
it. I mean, he notices some things that don't seem right—in this case,
the indulgences and their promise that you can buy forgiveness.
And when he points out these things to the authorities, he assumes
they'll want to fix them. And when they don't, he goes higher up.
And eventually there's no one higher to appeal to, because the pope
himself has excommunicated him. At each step, he is at best a reluc-
tant reformer, but he ultimately feels he has no choice.

"Captive to the word." So, it really is all because of what he finds in scripture?

Right, and in particular it's the grace of God granted through faith
that he finds in scripture. Ultimately, these insights lead him to
challenge almost all the established powers of his day and earn him
the title of "the monk who changed the world."

Like I said, it's a ton to take in.

Rest assured—if it seems like there's a lot to unpack, that's because
there is! Fortunately, we've got plenty of time to keep talking.

**Thanks. I appreciate that. Because I've still got a lot of questions. In fact, I
feel like I'm just getting started.**

I actually think that's a really good sign, and I'm happy to continue
the conversation.

Insights and Questions

CHAPTER 2

Freedom!

*Justification by Grace
through Faith*

So, you said that while you like the sound of what Luther was saying, you have a lot of questions.

Tons. In some ways, more than when we started. But maybe question number one right now is simply this: Why does it take Luther so long to get it through his head that God loves him? I mean, he seems like a pretty smart guy. And it sounds like he had already learned lots of theology. So what gives? Why does it take so long? Didn't anyone tell him this before?

That's a great question. One way to answer it would be to say that it isn't so much that Luther needs to learn *more* theology, but that he has absorbed a theology that's seriously inadequate, even if it is also kind of understandable.

Wait, inadequate and understandable? You've lost me.

I think Luther would say that theology, at its best, helps us understand God, even introduces us to God. And that was the problem: the theology of his day gave him a seriously deficient picture of God. That's what I mean by inadequate. But it's also understandable because this theology introduces him to the God most people expect. The God we tend to create for ourselves when we look around at the way the world works and try to deduce, or figure out, what God is like.

Okay, I'm still not with you. I appreciate you trying to explain this, but I need more to go on.

No worries, this isn't simple . . . until it is. Let me try it this way. When you look around at the way the world runs, what do you see?

Hmm?

What do you see? What do you notice? What are the rules of the world? How do things get done? That kind of thing.

I think it depends on where you're looking. When you look at nature, for instance, it's really beautiful, but also kind of dangerous. "Survival of the fittest" and all that. I mean, the strong and powerful seem to be in control. And it can be unpredictable—hurricanes, tornadoes, earthquakes. We're getting better and better at understanding how these things happen, but they still take us by surprise, sometimes with devastating results. So, I guess I'd say the natural world is beautiful but dangerous, with the advantage going to the strong.

The seventeenth-century philosopher Thomas Hobbes, in arguing why we need government, once described life in the natural world as "nasty, brutish, and short."[1]

That's a little more pessimistic than I would have put it, but I see his point.

Okay, so that's the natural world. What about the human or social world?

Well, it's similar, and more complex. In addition to beauty and danger, there's love and compassion too.

Definitely.

But there's also loneliness, I suppose, and heartache and pain and suffering. And power too, with "might making right" and so on. I guess the human world isn't all that much different from the natural world.

Now who's being pessimistic?

I'm just trying to be realistic.

I agree, and that is hugely important for understanding Luther, because he is, above all else, a realist. So you've said that both the natural and social worlds are beautiful but dangerous, unpredictable and complex, and places where power seems to dictate much of what goes on. Given all this, what kind of God would you deduce from this world? What kind of God, that is, does this world suggest?

Ah, I think I'm beginning to see what you mean. You might think that the God of this world is naturally a whole lot like the natural and social worlds: beautiful, awesome, powerful, unpredictable, and more than a little dangerous.

Right. And that's the way the theology of Luther's day tended to look at God—an all-powerful king to be worshiped, feared, and obeyed. God was loving, for sure, but also just, and it was the justice part that seemed to dominate the imagination of folks of that time.

Which is why Luther is obsessed with trying to make this God happy, by trying to do anything and everything he can think of to get right with this God. Because if you don't, you're in serious trouble.

Exactly, and eventually Luther comes to believe that this is the wrong way to picture God.

But it takes a while.

Yes. For most of us, it's not easy to unlearn things we grew up believing, and Luther is no exception.

So what makes the difference? What finally tips the balance?

Two things. The first is despair.

Despair?

Yup. Luther, as we mentioned earlier, tries and tries and tries to do everything he can to please this God of laws and demands and justice and punishment. But no matter how hard he tries, he is never sure he's successful. In fact, he's pretty sure he has failed miserably. And after a while, he actually grows to hate God.

Really?

Years later, he talked about how he felt at this time: "I did not love, yes, I hated the righteous God who punishes sinners, and secretly, if not blasphemously, certainly murmuring greatly, I was angry with God."[2]

Yikes. That couldn't have helped. I mean, it's bad enough to feel like you're falling short of God's standards; it's another altogether to hate God.

Exactly. And it's that sense of futility and despair that finally breaks down all the pictures of God Luther has carried with him since childhood, and opens him up to another way of seeing God. Which brings me to the second thing that tips the balance: scripture.

This is what you said before about Luther relying on the Bible alone—I think you called it *sola scriptura*?

Yes. Luther is reading and lecturing on the Bible at Wittenberg, and he keeps getting stuck on one line in particular while studying Paul's letter to the Romans: "The righteous will live by faith" (1:17, NIV). Based on the theology he'd inherited, Luther for years assumed this meant that those who lived just and righteous lives could trust—have faith—that God was pleased with them.

And since Luther wasn't righteous, that was not good news.

Right. But after trying so hard and for so long, and broken by that sense of futility and despair we just talked about, Luther realizes that he's been reading this verse backward. It's not that just and righteous people live by faith. It's that God makes us righteous, and all we can do is accept that in faith.

This sounds good, but I'd appreciate it if you'd say more.

Let me try it this way: up to this point, Luther believes that righteousness is God's *expectation*, the standard by which God judges us, and so righteousness is *our* responsibility. Eventually Luther realizes that righteousness isn't an expectation but instead is God's *gift* to us. That is, righteousness is *God's* responsibility and possession, and nothing pleases God more than to give that righteousness to us out of love. And once we realize that, we live trusting that God has made us righteous. This, in a nutshell, is Luther's major break-through: because God loves us, God justifies us by grace and we live into, accept, and actualize this righteousness by faith; that is, by trusting that God loves and redeems us.

That's a mouthful.

It certainly can be. The shorthand way to describe this central element of Luther's thought is to talk about "justification by grace through faith." That may be easier to remember.

"Justification by grace through faith." And the church of his day didn't buy this?

The church bought the part about grace, but also insisted that we obtain access to that grace by our works. Luther believes God takes responsibility for the whole thing: God is loving and God is gracious. And so God forgives us, accepts us, and declares us righteous. Period. Believing it is enough. No works on our part are necessary. Which is why, while the full term is "justification by grace through faith," through the years a lot of people have shortened it to "justification by faith." In fact, another rallying cry of the Reformation was *sola fide*—by "faith alone"!

***Sola fide. Sola scriptura.* Two "solas."**

Throw in *sola gratia*—by "grace alone"—and you've got a theological hat trick! For now, it's important to see just how strongly Luther believes that not only is God loving and gracious, but that simply accepting in faith that God forgives you makes it a reality in your life.

I like the sound of that. And, more importantly, I think I'm beginning to get this. I understand the part about God loving us instead of judging us, and that accepting God's forgiveness makes it real for us. But I'm still confused about this whole thing with righteousness. It seems like righteousness should be an objective thing. That is, there's this thing called the law, and the people who follow the law are righteous, and the people who don't follow it aren't. So how can righteousness be something that God gives us?

That's a great question. You're right, when we think of the word *righteous*, we normally think of it as being morally upright, more or less a synonym to "virtuous." But the word actually means "to be in right standing." And when it's used in the Bible, it means being in right standing with God.

Okay, I see what you mean. But each time we break the law, it seems we should no longer be in right standing with God.

Definitely.

And then we're no longer righteous, right? So how does God change that?

Let me put it this way. If someone you care about does something to hurt you, I'd imagine that they are no longer in right standing with you.

Sure.

And what happens then?

What do you mean?

When someone is no longer in right standing with you, what happens? Does the relationship end? Is it over? Do you never have anything to do with the person again?

Occasionally, but honestly not all that often. Usually I move beyond it. The person either apologizes or I forgive them or both.

Right. And that's what God does.

Interesting. So being righteous isn't so much about *morality*—getting everything right—as it is about *relationship*—being in right relationship with someone. And in this case, that's God.

That's a nice way of putting it.

So this is what you meant by saying that righteousness is *God's* responsibility and possession, something God can give us. Because it's ultimately up to God to decide whether we're in right relationship with God, in the same way that it's ultimately up to me to decide whether I will allow someone who has disappointed me to be in right relationship with me.

Exactly.

Okay, I think I'm beginning to get this. And I like it. But, to be honest, it's going to take a little while for it all to sink in.

No worries—it took Luther a long time too.

I mean, I like the way it sounds, but it also feels like there's something not quite right about it all.

Interesting. What do you mean?

Well, I'm glad God forgives us, but it kind of seems like God shouldn't. I know that sounds awful, but I guess what I'm saying is that if God forgives us, then why should we behave?

That reminds me of when my sister broke the news to her ten-year-old son that there was no Santa Claus and, after thinking about it for a minute, he responded grumpily, "I guess there's no reason to be good this year!"

Exactly. If God isn't going to punish us for being bad or reward us for being good, what's the point? Or at least what's the motivation for trying to be good?

That brings us right back to our conversation earlier about the theology we're born with—or at least the theology we derive from our observations of nature—and how that usually results in a distorted picture of God.

How so?

You've essentially said God is primarily about rewards and punishments. And if your only source of knowledge about God is the natural world, that makes sense, because the natural world seems to run according to cause and effect: do good things, get rewarded; do bad things, get punished. But that leads to a distorted sense of God.

Kind of like a twisted version of Santa Claus.

Say again?

Your story about your nephew reminded me of the line from "Santa Claus Is Coming to Town": "He sees you when you're sleeping. He knows when you're awake. He knows if you've been bad or good, so be good for goodness' sake!"

> Got it. Yes, that's the kind of picture of God you end up with when you only look at the world—a God who makes a lot of rules and then sits up in heaven watching to make sure we all follow them . . . or else.

And that's what Luther grew up with, until he realizes that God is a God of love and, out of love, God forgives us when we screw up, which puts us back in right standing with God.

> You've got it!

Okay. I like that, even if it does take some getting used to. But I still wonder about one thing.

> Go ahead.

Doesn't this make the law kind of weak? Even if God is loving instead of judging, doesn't God want us to follow the law? And if God forgives us when we don't, doesn't that make it less likely we'll bother following the law? I mean, isn't the threat of punishment essential to taking the law seriously? And if there are no consequences for breaking the law, doesn't that undermine our notions of justice?

> These are good questions. We should spend some more time talking about how Luther understands God's law. But for now, let me go back to something you said earlier.

Okay.

> You said that when someone has hurt or disappointed you, most often you find a way forward. Either the person apologizes or you forgive him or her, or both.

That's right.

> How often does punishment come into play?

Punishment? Uh, not often. I mean, I'm not exactly in a position to punish someone with jail time or something like that just because I've been hurt or disappointed by something they did.

True. But you could punish them in other ways. You could withhold your friendship. You could not talk to them again. You could try to hurt them back.

Maybe. And that probably does happen sometimes. You feel hurt, so you don't talk to the person for a while. But I don't know if I'd call that punishment. It's more like consequences.

That's fair. There are consequences to our actions. But ultimately you have to decide whether to continue in the relationship. And if you do, the only way forward, it seems to me, is by forgiveness. And forgiveness introduces a different kind of logic from justice.

Can you say more?

Sure. Let's say we decide that we're going to live entirely according to a sense of justice, where every infraction of the law demands restitution, punishment, or at least some kind of consequences.

Okay.

What does that do to our personal relationships? I mean, we may want to set up society that way—you speed and you get a ticket, and so on—but what happens to your relationships with your family and friends if you live strictly by this sense of justice?

You mean what would happen if I made sure every time a friend or family member did something wrong to me, I would not continue in the relationship until they'd paid the price? And I assume the reverse would have to be true as well. That is, every time I did something wrong—big or little—there would have to be some kind of reckoning?

Yes.

I think I see where you're going. Life would be miserable. Constantly checking up on each other. Constantly making sure everything was accounted for and everyone got whatever they were due. Constantly making sure there were consequences for everything that happened. Maybe things would be fairer, but I don't see how you could stay in relationship with anybody. In fact, I think you'd end up hating each other in the name of justice. It would be horrible.

And that's why forgiveness is so essential. While we live in a world of laws for the sake of justice, forgiveness makes it possible for us to live in that world without being crushed by it.

Interesting. Can you say more?

Forgiveness introduces something new. It interrupts the law of cause and effect. Jesus at one point says something quite similar. In his Sermon on the Mount, Jesus says, "You have heard that it was said, 'An eye for an eye and a tooth for a tooth.' But I say to you, do not resist an evildoer. But if anyone strikes you on the right cheek, turn the other also; and if anyone wants to sue you and take your coat, give your cloak as well; and if anyone forces you to go one mile, go also the second mile" (Matthew 5:38–41). Some people think that in saying this, Jesus is making the law even harder to follow, but I think it shows that as important as the law is, there are limits.

It reminds me of a quote from Gandhi: "An eye for an eye leaves the whole world blind."

Exactly. Without forgiveness and the opportunity it creates to do a new thing, we can't bear to live in the world together.

Again, I find that really interesting. It's making more and more sense to me. I began by wondering what motivation there is to follow the law if forgiveness is possible, but now I see that, without the possibility of forgiveness, the world of law and order crushes you.

Which is exactly how Luther feels—crushed by the law and ultimately redeemed, empowered, and set free by the gospel, the good news of God's love, grace, and forgiveness.

Thanks for taking the time to explain all this. I have a better sense of what you mean by saying Luther comes to believe his theology is inadequate even if it is understandable.

Right, and because theology helps us picture God, this new theological lens introduces him to a "new" God—or at least a new picture of God—whom he meets by reading scripture. And that new picture of God's grace, mercy, and love changes how Luther sees nearly everything: theology, God, the church, our life together in the world, you name it.

I think I'm beginning to see why Luther's insight means so much to him. I mean, after all those years trying to do everything right, trying so hard to be acceptable, and feeling like he never, ever quite succeeded, it must have been a huge relief to discover that God had, as you said, already done everything for him.

Luther later described it as having the gates of heaven open up to him.

Makes sense. If you'd felt that level of despair and hopelessness, I can only imagine how important this was. But I'm still curious about something.

What's that?

Given the way Luther feels about indulgences, and given this huge insight that changes pretty much everything about how he sees God, and given that he starts a church—even if he didn't want it named after himself—well, after all this, does he still think of himself as a devout Roman Catholic?

I'd put it this way: especially in the early part of his career, Luther definitely thinks that he's still a faithful Roman Catholic. Like I said, he isn't trying to do anything new. He's trying to help the church get back to its essential message. But at the same time, even though he feels he's still part of the church, he also feels like he's now practicing a somewhat different religion from the one he'd grown up in.

Whoa. A different religion? A different picture of God I understand, but did that really change his religion?

Maybe it would be more accurate to say that Luther feels he's getting back to practicing the original faith of the church, the faith described in the New Testament and taught by Jesus. But to do that, he has to criticize the version of Christianity that is popular in his day. The version that stressed God's judgment over God's love, set up the church as the mediator between God and humans, and made God's promises conditional by requiring human works.

Okay, the part about getting back to the original message of Jesus makes sense. But I'd still appreciate it if you'd say more about how that's different than what the church of his day was saying.

Maybe this will help. Think, for a minute, about elevators.

Elevators?

Yup. What do they do?

Uh, they go up and down.

Precisely. And Luther realizes that the version of the Christian faith of his day is confused about elevators. Of course, they didn't have elevators in the sixteenth century! But there is confusion about the primary direction or focus of the Christian life.

Hmm, still not with you.

According to the church of Luther's day, the primary work of the Christian is to get back up to God.

"Back up to God"?

Yeah. The idea was that in the beginning, God and humans—represented by Adam and Eve—enjoyed perfect community with each other. But then humans blew it by sinning.

The whole "forbidden fruit" incident. We talked about this a bit already.

Right. Central to the story is that God gave Adam and Eve all these great things to eat and a wonderful place to live and all the rest. And all God expected of them was to not eat the fruit of the tree of the knowledge of good and evil.

But they did.

Yes. And for centuries this story has been called "the fall." As in Adam and Eve fell from grace, and that has been our condition ever since. In response, the medieval church focused most of its energies on providing ways for humans to climb back into God's good graces. That was the goal, and they could reach it by doing good works, by making donations to the church, by becoming a monk or nun, by going on Crusades . . .

Or by purchasing indulgences.

Right.

But Luther believes we don't have to work to get back into God's good graces. That because being in good standing is primarily a relational thing, God can forgive us and restore us to right relationship.

Right again.

Which is why Luther challenges indulgences.

Exactly. When he reads scripture carefully, Luther sees that the biblical witness places its faith not in our ability to *earn* God's favor but in God's promise to *give* us God's good favor.

All of that from just reading the Bible?

And a pretty good dose of despair and ample prayer!

Okay, but I still don't quite get the elevator analogy.

Thanks—almost forgot about that! Well, we might describe the theology we've been talking about as an "up" religion, as everything is geared toward climbing back up to God. According to some scholars, that's more or less what the word "religion" means.

Say again?

The Latin word *ligare* means "to bind." That same root word is at the heart of our word "ligament." In a sense, some say religion is the means we use in trying to attach—or in this case reattach—ourselves to God.

And Luther doesn't go for that?

Nope. Through both his own experience and his reading of the Bible, Luther feels that we are ultimately incapable of closing the gap between God and ourselves.

Which means "up" religion doesn't work.

More than that, by working so hard to get back up to God, we actually miss God's continual movement to come down to us.

Down?

These are spatial metaphors, of course. Lutheran theologian Gerhard Forde is known for expressing Luther's theology in this way. Lots of people, when they picture heaven, think of it as being "up there." So if you think of God up in heaven, then all the while we're trying to climb *up* to God, God is determined to come *down* to us, to meet us where we are.

I think I'm following, but say more.

Luther feels that, because God loves us, God does what we can't. God closes the gap created by sin. In this sense, God comes *down* to meet us just where we are. So, in contrast to the "up" religion that we are born with, Luther invites us to imagine a "down" religion that focuses, not on all the things we have to do, but on what God has already done for us by coming down to meet us.

This is beginning to fall into place.

And the two primary places in the biblical story that God comes down to meet us are in the incarnation and the cross.

Why those two?

The incarnation because in Jesus' birth the eternal Word of God takes on human flesh—is incarnated—to become one of us (John 1:14). Luther sees the incarnation as a supreme act of accommodation—being born as a vulnerable baby to become one of us.

That makes sense and certainly captures the sense of God coming down to us. But why the cross?

If Jesus' birth is God becoming one of us, then the cross is God joining *all* of human life, including death. Moreover, it's not just any death, but an unfair, even unjust, death. In this sense, the cross represents God's willing embrace of all of human life: laughter, joy, hope, community, and more, but also tears, pain, injustice, isolation, and death. In both the manger and the cross, God becomes as vulnerable as we are.

Got it. That actually doesn't just make sense, it's comforting. That God knows what it's like to be afraid or alone, to hurt or to feel despair.

Luther thinks so too, and he feels that "up religion," because it focuses on God's holiness and glory and all the things we have to do to measure up, distracts us from recognizing God's love and, from that love, God's commitment to meet us where we actually are, not waiting until we deserve God's attention and care, but lavishing it on us as we are.

Like ships passing in the night.

Or elevators missing each other as one goes up and the other goes down.

We work
to get back
"UP" to GOD.

GOD
comes "down"
to us.

Elevators, right. Okay, now I've finally got the elevator thing. It sounds like Luther fears that focusing on what we have to do makes it hard to realize how much God has already done for us out of love.

Exactly. In his letter to the Romans, Paul puts it this way, "For while we were still weak, at the right time Christ died for the ungodly.

Indeed, rarely will anyone die for a righteous person—though perhaps for a good person someone might actually dare to die. But God proves his love for us in that while we still were sinners Christ died for us" (Romans 5:6–8).

Wow. That pretty much captures it. And it brings us back to what you said earlier about all of this introducing Luther to a different picture of God.

Right.

It's hard to understand how people overlook verses like that one.

I'm not so sure. I know what you mean in the sense that what Paul wrote to the Romans seems pretty clear that God loves us. But I also think it's easier for us to miss than we might think.

Why?

Part of the reason is what we've been talking about with "up religion." It seems like so much of the natural and, for that matter, the social worlds are governed by "survival of the fittest." It's easy to assume that the world is inherently competitive and figure God is like that too, always judging us or expecting us to make the grade, and so on. But I also think it may be part of human nature to assume that the burden is on us to prove ourselves worthy. To feel pressure to justify ourselves. To wonder if we deserve being loved.

Really?

Well, for example, how often do you assume you'll be liked and admired when you meet a group of strangers? Or on a day-to-day basis, how often do you feel just great about yourself—your looks, your body, your intelligence, your achievements? How often, that is, do you feel like you're just plain *enough*?

Great questions, but also painful. Because even though, on the whole, I'm a pretty happy, even confident person, there are a lot of times when I feel kind of insecure about whether I'm doing enough or even if I *am* enough. Though I don't talk about it all that often.

Most of us don't. But I think that's just part of what it is to be human. And that's what the biblical story affirms too.

How so?

Well, remember when we talked about Adam and Eve and their "fall from grace"?

Sure.

When you read that story closely, it's pretty much all about Adam and Eve's insecurity. I mean, the only reason the serpent can tempt them into taking the fruit is by first making sure they feel like they're missing out on something. Like somehow their life with each other and with God isn't enough. That they are inadequate, insufficient, unacceptable. Once the serpent has done that, all he has to do is offer the fruit as the solution to all their problems.

Interesting. He makes them feel insecure and then tells them that by breaking God's commandment they'll find the remedy for their insecurity.

In this sense, I think that original insecurity comes before original sin. And I don't think it stopped with Adam and Eve.

What do you mean?

Well, we've already mentioned that it's really hard for most of us to accept ourselves as adequate or sufficient. I think that's because insecurity is just part of being human. But I also think our culture multiplies that insecurity incessantly, even exploits it.

In what way?

Think about all the ads you see in any given day. It doesn't matter where—print, radio, television, Internet. What do most of them have in common?

They're all trying to sell me something.

Right. And have you ever noticed how they do that? How do they get you to believe you need their product? What kind of feeling do they create in you?

Ah, I see what you mean. They most often create a sense of lack, like I'm missing something or have a problem: hair loss, or being overweight, or having acne, or teeth that aren't brilliantly white, or whatever.

Right.

What's interesting is you never think to question what's the big deal about acne or less than blindingly white teeth. You just assume it's the worst thing ever and need to do something about it.

Exactly. And sometimes the ads don't show you problems at all but instead show you perfect people leading perfect lives with perfect jobs and perfect children and all the rest.

Right. And by watching all this "perfectness," you end up feeling like a perfect slob, totally unfit to go out in public!

Hopefully not quite that bad!

Probably not. But bad enough. I mean, think about how few of us—if any of us these days—feel good about our looks and our bodies. I think a lot of it comes from comparing ourselves to the perfect people we see in ads, forgetting all the time that no one looks like that.

As in *absolutely* no one. Most pictures in magazines are of people who've spent all this time getting made up for the photos, are shown in perfect lighting and shot by professional photographers, and the pictures are later airbrushed to hide any blemishes. That is, to hide anything truly human.

Right. Although it feels like we're being pretty hard on advertisers.

Advertisers are just trying to sell their products, and they've realized they can do their job better by exploiting our insecurities. But in the end, it's not about advertisements per se, it's about how insecure we are and all the things we'll do to ourselves and others to make ourselves less insecure.

Like what?

Sometimes we figure we need to change ourselves to be acceptable. Become thinner or smarter or younger looking or whatever. Or maybe we try to become more acceptable to the people around us by fitting in.

In which case, you start from the premise that you're not enough and you need to do something about it.

I'd say that's another form of trying to justify yourself. It's not by doing good works to earn God's approval, as with Luther, but it is by doing "good works" of another kind to gain the approval of those around you.

I hadn't thought of it that way. And, to be honest, that helps a lot. Because while I find it pretty cool that Luther goes from thinking God is out to get him to seeing that God is totally for him, I wonder how relevant that insight is for us today.

You mean you don't spend most of your waking hours wondering whether God is merciful?

Uh, not really.

I don't think too many people do.

But I do spend plenty of time wondering whether I'm good enough. Whether I'll measure up or be okay or deserve to be loved and all the rest. I hadn't thought of that as an attempt to justify myself.

That's a big part of the reason I find Luther's insight so helpful. It reminds me that, according to God, I'm totally enough. That I don't need to change to merit God's love or attention. That God is still coming down to meet me where I am and accept me as I am.

That's really powerful.

And what's just as powerful is that as soon as I realize God is doing that for me, I realize God's doing it for everybody else as well.

What do you mean?

Well, I don't think the pressure to justify ourselves stops with us being hard on ourselves. I think it makes us hard on everyone else too.

Say more.

When you feel like you always have to measure up, it's easy, as we said, to feel like life is one big competition. And, all of a sudden, the people around you aren't colleagues and friends and partners, they're . . .

Competitors for whatever you're hoping to find—acceptance or love or a sense of being worthy or whatever.

Exactly. And before long you're judging people for all kinds of things to make yourself feel better about yourself.

Out of insecurity. I get it. It's like life is one long episode of *"Survivor"* or some other reality TV show, where we're constantly putting other people down to get ahead.

Right. So whether you're trying to measure up or putting others down . . .

You're still trying to justify yourself. To make yourself feel worthy or acceptable, whether to yourself, to those around you, or to God.

In his book *Life Together*, the German theologian and martyr Dietrich Bonhoeffer said that "self-justification and judging go together, just as justification by grace and serving others go together."[3]

That's cool. And I think that goes a long way toward explaining prejudice.

Interesting. Would you mind saying more?

Well, you got me thinking. The essence of prejudice is judging someone else not on what they do or who they really are, but who you *think* they are. You don't even get to know them. You decide ahead of time that because of their race or gender or age or ethnicity or whatever, they're not good enough. And now that we're talking about it, it just seems like a lot of that is out of insecurity and fear. You are prejudiced—or at least you're insecure and fearful enough to become prejudiced—because you don't think there's enough to go around. Whatever the "enough" is—money, prestige, influence, jobs, land, social capital—and so you find reasons to look down on people you've come to see as competitors.

I think that's really insightful.

It's intriguing to me that some of what Luther said five hundred years ago helps me explain things today.

I totally agree. And here's the thing: Luther, a medieval Christian living in sixteenth-century Germany, was very worried about whether God is merciful or vengeful. Not many people are burdened by that same question. But beneath his very contextual question is a set of much larger concerns: How do we know we're acceptable? Where do we find a place to stand? What does it mean to be human? What is the meaning of life?

Which is what I find really interesting—that we're still struggling with these same questions, at least the big questions about what it means to be human.

Exactly.

So, can we go back to what Bonhoeffer said? Especially the second part, because I think that's one of those big questions. I completely get the part about how self-justification leads to judging. But how do we go from justification by grace to serving others?

I think this works in two ways. First, if you feel better about yourself—like you're okay and acceptable and totally enough as you are—then it's a whole lot easier to share those good feelings with others. By being acceptable, you've already kind of won, so life isn't a competition anymore and you don't have to view the people around you as competitors, but just people who may need a little help.

That makes sense. And because you know what a difference acceptance has made to you, and because you feel accepted, maybe it's easier to accept others.

Exactly. Second, you've also now suddenly got a lot of time on your hands.

Uh, I'm not sure what you mean.

So we talked about how much time and energy we put into trying to justify ourselves. Suddenly, you don't have to worry about that. Why not put some of that extra time and energy into caring for the people around you?

I honestly hadn't thought about it that way.

To go back to spatial metaphors for a moment: "Up religion" requires you to put all your energy into fixing what we might call your *vertical* relationship with God. Luther's—or really the Bible's—emphasis on God coming down to meet us means you don't have to worry about that anymore, so you are free to focus on what we might call your *horizontal* relationships with the people around you. It's like God saying, "Let me take care of the really big questions like, say, your worth as a human being and your eternal destiny, so you're now free to love the people around you."

I can see how this would seem freeing, and how it would draw you closer to the people around you to help them.

One of the things Luther never got tired of repeating captures it well: "God does not need our good works, but our neighbor does."[4]

That's really cool. I think most people think being religious is all about doing, well, religious things to make God happy, so I especially love the idea that the Christian faith actually frees you to not worry about God and instead take care of the people around you.

That's exactly right. Luther is essentially all about freedom. Freedom from and freedom for.

Say again?

First, you're freed *from* worrying about your relationship with God, then you're freed *for* a life of meaning and purpose dedicated to loving and caring for the people all around you.

I really like that.

It's not always that easy of course. We struggle to believe we've been forgiven. We have a hard time loving our neighbor the way we should. Nevertheless, God is still all about freedom, the freedom that comes from knowing you are loved, forgiven, and have value.

Freedom from and freedom for. Yeah, this is beginning to really sink in.

I'm glad this is making sense.

Me too. But what's next?

What do you mean?

I'm enjoying understanding how Luther's thought helps make sense of our life today, and I'm wondering what we might take up next.

Well, since we're talking about how justification by grace frees you to take care of your neighbor, we could talk about how Luther thinks this happens. You might like that, because it's another example of Luther calling into question some of our assumptions about what it means to be a Christian, in order to set us loose to care for the people around us.

Great. Let's go there next.

Insights and Questions

CHAPTER 3

The Present-Tense God
Law and Gospel

Okay, I'm ready to be surprised.

Really?

Well, you said Luther has more to say about how we can take care of each other and that some of his thoughts on this might call into question some of our assumptions about what it means to be religious. So I'm ready to be surprised.

Got it. Actually, I think I said he might call into question what we think it means to be a *Christian*, not simply religious.

There's a difference?

As we said earlier, the Latin word at the root of religion is *ligare*, which means "to bind or attach." Religion, in this sense, is a means by which to attach ourselves to God.

And Luther is not in favor of that, because it focuses on what we have to do to get back in God's good graces instead of realizing how much God has already done to take care of that and to free us to care for our neighbor.

Right. Luther doesn't think of Christianity primarily as a set of rules or doctrines for getting in good standing with God. Rather, he understands it as a set of relationships: a relationship with God that God takes responsibility for, and relationships with each other for which we have responsibility.

What you earlier called our vertical relationship with God and horizontal relationships with each other.

Yup.

That all seems straightforward. I mean, it's not necessarily what you'd expect because, as we said, it seems to be part of human nature to be insecure and think it's up to us to justify ourselves. But once you get that God comes down to us in love to give us a sense of worth and dignity, it's pretty cool and makes a lot of sense. So where do we go from here?

Well, since we're talking about what God does for us, I think it might be helpful to talk about one other thing God does for us that helps us to love and care for each other.

Sounds good.

And that is to give us the law as a gift.

Law? As in "law and order"? As in "do this" or "don't do that or else"?

Yes.

Uh, okay. But I'll be honest, it doesn't sound all that much like a gift.

What makes you say that?

Just that laws usually make you nervous. They feel kind of threatening. And when you break them, they're definitely not fun.

I think you're probably not alone in that opinion. But I'd like to invite you to reconsider.

Sure, I'll give it a try.

Great. A little while ago, you said people who follow the law are righteous and those who don't follow it aren't.

I remember that.

Here's where we can start reconsidering things. Because, interestingly, in the Bible, the law isn't given to make us righteous.

Really? Then what's it for?

I'll get to that in a second. But, first, I'm curious about what made you assume that following the law is the way we become righteous. Keep in mind that I think most people think this way.

Well, I guess it seems like the law tells us what we're supposed to do, what God wants us to do. So, if we keep the law, then we're doing what God wants us to do and are more or less righteous. Although, to be honest, I don't think many people use that word any more. We'd probably just say that keeping the law makes you a good person. Although . . .

Yes?

I remember that earlier we said that righteousness isn't so much about morality as it is about relationships. That's why God can justify us or make us righteous, because it's up to God to say who's in good standing with God. Is that part of where we're going?

Definitely. On the one hand, you're absolutely right. The law tells us what God wants from us, even what God expects from us. But keeping or not keeping the law isn't about being righteous or getting in God's good graces or making God happy or any of that. In fact, I'd say it's pretty much just the opposite.

How so?

I'd say—or, really, the biblical story says—that the law isn't given by God to help us make God happy or to help us become righteous. Rather, because God is *already* happy with us and has *already* declared us righteous, God gives us the law as a gift.

Well, that's definitely not what I expected. I said I was looking forward to being surprised. But, to be honest, I'm not totally sure I'm following you.

No problem. Let's go to a biblical story to illustrate it.

Sounds good.

This time, we'll go to the Exodus story.

As in "exodus" in the movies?

Yup.

Cool. I've seen nearly all the "exodus" movies: Charlton Heston in *The Ten Commandments* (Paramount, 1956), Christian Bale in *Exodus: Gods and Kings* (Fox, 2014), and the animated *Prince of Egypt* (DreamWorks, 1998).

Then you're definitely ahead of me. I didn't even know there were three versions. Which was your favorite?

Either *The Ten Commandments* or *Prince of Egypt*. I like Christian Bale, but didn't think the movie was so great. And, now that you mention it, it's kind of interesting they keep telling that story.

There are central dramas in the Bible that people keep telling because they're pivotal stories, not only in the Bible but also in our human history, culture, and experience. And this is definitely one of them. After seeing the films, you probably remember the basic plot line of the story.

Sure. The Israelites are slaves in Egypt, and God sends Moses to lead them to safety. And, after lots of arguing with the Pharaoh, plagues, and crossing the Red Sea, Moses does it. He brings the people out of Egypt.

Right, and I want to focus on the scenes right after that.

The part when God gives the ten commandments?

Right. And here's where it gets interesting. In the biblical story, God has already made a covenant with the people of Israel before God gives them the law.

Let's slow down for a minute. Covenant?

Yeah. Kind of like a binding promise of relationship. God essentially tells the people of Israel that they will be God's people, and God will take care of them and be their God.

Okay, that's more or less what I thought. But why does it matter that the covenant is made *before* God gives the ten commandments?

Because if God wanted to give the Israelites—and here, by extension, all of us—the law to help us *become* God's people, or become righteous or earn God's good graces or however we want to phrase it, God would give the law first.

I see what you mean. Then the law would be like an instruction manual on how to be righteous and earn God's favor.

Exactly. But God makes the covenant first—essentially showing the Israelites that they are *already* God's people, no matter what.

Which means God gives the Israelites the law not to *become* God's people but because they are God's people *already*.

Right again! And, in fact, much of the rest of the story describes Israel breaking God's law over and over again, but they never stop being God's people.

All of which goes to show that the law really is a gift to people God has already accepted, not a set of instructions to become acceptable or get back to God.

And when you read closely, you discover that most of the law actually has little to do with God. Which brings us back to your question about what the law is for, if it's not about becoming righteous.

And . . . ?

Actually, I think you can probably figure it out. If the law isn't our manual on dealing with our vertical relationship with God, then . . .

It's about our horizontal relationships with each other.

Precisely. And that's what Luther discovers when he reads the ten commandments.

Can you say more?

Well, the ten commandments aren't the whole of the law in the Bible, but they represent the heart of the law. And while the first few are about our relationship with God, the majority are about the people who live around us. Maybe it would be helpful to turn to the passage in Exodus that describes the giving of the law.

Sounds good.

This is from the twentieth chapter of Exodus, just after God has promised to be the people's God and declared Israel to be God's people.

Then God spoke all these words:

I am the LORD your God, who brought you out of the land of Egypt, out of the house of slavery; you shall have no other gods before me.

You shall not make for yourself an idol, whether in the form of anything that is in heaven above, or that is on the earth beneath, or that is in the water under the earth. You shall not bow down to them or worship them; for I the LORD your God am a jealous God, punishing children for the iniquity of parents, to the third and the fourth generation of those who reject me, but showing steadfast love to the thousandth generation of those who love me and keep my commandments.

You shall not make wrongful use of the name of the LORD your God, for the LORD will not acquit anyone who misuses his name.

Remember the sabbath day, and keep it holy. For six days you shall labor and do all your work. But the seventh day is a sabbath to the LORD your God; you shall not do any work—you, your son or your daughter, your male or female slave, your livestock, or the alien resident in your towns. For in six days the LORD made heaven and earth, the sea, and all that is in them, but rested the seventh day; therefore, the LORD blessed the sabbath day and consecrated it.

Honor your father and your mother, so that your days may be long in the land that the LORD your God is giving you.

You shall not murder.

You shall not commit adultery.

You shall not steal.

You shall not bear false witness against your neighbor.

You shall not covet your neighbor's house; you shall not covet your neighbor's wife, or male or female slave, or ox, or donkey, or anything that belongs to your neighbor. (Exodus 20:1–17)

Quite a list.

What do you notice?

What do you mean?

I think one of the best ways to read the Bible is simply to pay attention to what you notice. To what sticks out or gets your attention or causes a reaction or raises questions. The folks who wrote, collected, and edited these stories were, among other things, artists. They were trying to make an impression with their testimony, and so one great way into these passages is simply to pay attention to what you notice, trusting that it's probably not an accident. So . . . what do you notice?

Well, first off, we talk about these as commandments, but the first one starts out with a reminder of who God is and what God has done—delivered the people out of Egypt—before getting to the commandment about not having other gods.

And what do you make of that?

I think it goes back to this idea about relationships. God starts out reminding the people of the relationship they have.

And why do you think the commandments start out with that reminder of relationship?

Probably so the people know they can trust God, and maybe also to root all the commandments in this relationship. That is, God's not just out making rules to impose God's power or authority, but because God loves them and wants the best for them.

I think you're probably right. What else do you notice?

Well, the next couple of commandments seem to follow from the first. I mean, if God is really your God and you're not going to follow other gods, then you're not going to make idols. Likewise, if God is really your God, then you're not going to "make wrongful use of the name of the Lord." I'm not totally sure what that means, but these first commandments seem to go together.

Luther would say that not making wrongful use of the Lord's name is about honoring God's name, not using it to justify doing bad things, not using it to swear to things you don't believe, not using it to deceive someone—like saying, "It's the honest-to-God truth" when you know it's a lie. Essentially, you're right. These first few commandments pretty much all go together.

By the way, how many commandments did we just cover? I'm confused about how we're supposed to number them.

You're not alone. Different traditions number the commandments differently. In the end, it's probably easiest to divide them between what's sometimes called the first table—the commandments connected to our relationship with God—and the second table—the commandments that deal with our relationships with each other.

Okay, let's go with that. Like I said, the ones dealing with God pretty much all go together and essentially say the same thing: if God is going to be your God, then you should mean it. That is, don't take other gods, don't make idols of other gods, don't misuse God's name. Which should bring us to the second table, the ones about how we are to treat each other. But before we go to that, I'm not sure what to do with the commandment about the sabbath.

What do you mean?

Well, that's about Sunday, right?

For the Israelites who received these commandments, and for all the Jewish people who followed them, this actually is *Saturday*, the seventh day of the week. Christians end up focusing more on Sunday because that's the day on which God raised Jesus from the dead. So, for our purposes, we can talk about sabbath as Sunday.

Okay. So is keeping the sabbath holy about God—the day we're supposed to set aside for honoring God? Or is it somehow more about how we treat each other?

Well, the primary description of the sabbath is that it is a day of rest. The Exodus passage references the creation story, saying that just as God rested after working six days, everyone else should get a day of rest too.

Sounds reasonable.

It was actually considered not just reasonable but crucial. Keep in mind that these words are directed to people who had only recently been slaves. Which means they didn't get to rest—ever. And so this comes as incredibly good news to them. God is essentially guaranteeing time to rest to these former slaves by making it a commandment.

Interesting.

And you can tell how important it is because *everyone* gets to rest. Adults, children, servants, animals, visitors. Everyone needs a break, a chance to rest and be renewed.

To be honest, I've not thought about it this way before. Usually, I think it just means you ought to go to church. And to make sure people went to church, there was even a time when nothing else was open on Sundays. So I guess this has always felt pretty old-fashioned to me.

I think going to church is what this has come to mean for most people. And, frankly, I can understand the motivation for interpreting it that way, even if we don't read it that way anymore. I mean, church is the place where you hear about God's love. And because that's a message we don't necessarily expect, it can be hard to believe. And so making space to hear the good news matters. On the whole, I think the commandment is stressing the importance of setting aside a day for rest, renewal, and remembering how much God loves us.

Then it's definitely more about us than about God. And it might just be one of the more important commandments right now.

What do you mean?

Just that it feels like no one really rests any more, like there is no sabbath. For a lot of people I know, work feels endless. Thanks to email, most of us can now work at night, work on the weekend, whenever. It's like there's no break at all.

I know what you mean. There's no getting away.

Which is kind of ironic. When email first arrived on the scene, everyone thought it was going to be this great timesaver, but now all it does is make it almost impossible to ever take a break. Even when I go on vacation, I feel like I have these two unsavory choices: either check email every other day—so I never get away—or don't check, but start dreading the crazy amount of email I'll have to answer when I get back.

So maybe having a commandment to rest makes more sense than we thought?

Yeah. It definitely makes me think differently. Take stores being closed or open on Sundays, for instance. On the one hand, I suppose if going shopping is restful, a way for you to take a break, something you don't get to do during the week, then why not shop? On the other hand, when do the people who work at stores get a break? I'm not sure I'd want to go back to a time when everything was closed on Sundays, but I do think it's important that we find some way to rest.

And that, I think, is the heart of the commandments: to see them not as a list of "dos and don'ts" but instead to recognize that God cares enough about us to give us commandments that will make our lives together better. And Luther would invite us to have a rather dynamic, even creative, relationship with the law.

How so?

Well, it's like you just mentioned. Maybe people can rest on the sabbath, maybe not. The point isn't sticking to the letter of the law but rather sensing the underlying principle or value it expresses and finding ways to make that more of a reality in our own lives and in the lives of those around us—like making sure everyone has a chance to rest.

Which brings us to the second table of the commandments, because it's clearly about taking care of each other. Which, I have to say, is again surprising.

Why?

Well, as I mentioned, we tend to think of laws as negative. In part that's because it's no fun getting caught breaking a law. And in part it's because the commandments are worded negatively: "thou shalt not" and all that. But when you think about it, they're all about taking care of the people around you.

> Luther, referring to Jesus' parable about the good Samaritan, talks about the Christian's responsibility to take care of your neighbor, understanding "neighbor" to be not just the person next door but the person in need.

Exactly. And so while they come across as negative—not killing each other, not lying to each other, not wanting each other's stuff—they're actually quite positive. In a sense, they say, "Thou shalt take care of each other!" So negative command, but positive outcome.

> I think you're exactly right. And Luther would agree too. In fact, when he explains the commandments, he always names the positive outcome or positive force of each one, which is an example of his dynamic, creative relationship to the law. So the commandment about not bearing false witness against your neighbor, for instance, isn't only about not slandering or lying about your neighbors but also about speaking positively about them and even putting the best construction on what they say and do.

Sounds like a good commandment for social media, where people seem to want to jump down everyone else's throat about almost everything.

> Again, for Luther, this is what the commandments do. They make it possible for us to live with each other, because they demand we treat each other in a civil manner. In fact, he talks about what he calls the *first* or *civil* use of the law in just these terms.

I'm not sure I follow.

> Law isn't theoretical. As you've said a couple of times, it does things, it acts on us, which is why it can feel negative when it's keeping us from doing something that, even if it's wrong, we still want to do.

Like driving above the speed limit.

> Exactly. Not a good feeling to be pulled over by a state trooper, but . . .

Definitely helpful in keeping people safe.

And that's an example of a "use" of the law—to protect people from someone who drives recklessly. Because Luther thinks these laws create the possibility for civilization, he talks about this as the "civil use of the law."

But you also said he calls it the "first use of the law."

Yes. Luther believes there are two uses of the law. The first encourages us—and sometimes forces us—to be civil by setting rules, boundaries, and consequences that both keep us from doing whatever we want and direct us to care for each other. The second use of the law functions differently, as it creates in us the awareness of our need for God.

Okay, let's slow down. How does it do that?

In short, the law points out that we've done something wrong, which in turn highlights that we need God and, in particular, God's grace. Luther calls it the *theological use of the law* because it reminds us that we aren't perfect and creates in us the desire to receive God's grace and forgiveness.

And this is what you experience when you feel bad about something?

That's part of it, but really just a part of it. Certainly, the law is there so when you know you've done something wrong, you usually experience some sense of sorrow, regret, or guilt. And I'd say that's important, particularly when you remember that most of the law is devoted to helping us care for each other. When we break the law, we aren't doing that abstractly, we're often actually hurting others. And just like we teach our children, when you hurt someone you should regret that and apologize.

I agree.

And even when we don't actually hurt someone when we break the law, we're still risking the chance that we will.

So in our example of driving over the speed limit, even if I don't run into someone while speeding, I still risk doing that. That's why the law is there, to discourage us from speeding. But that's the first use of the law, right?

Right. Each year in the United States, more than 40,000 people die in traffic accidents, many related to speeding. So, whether or not you hit someone, you certainly could. The law in its first use tries to prevent this by restraining your desire to look out for yourself rather than your neighbor.

Then where does the second use come in?

While the first and second use are connected, they're also distinct. The first use, as we've been saying, tries to keep us from hurting others and, more positively, directs us to take care of them. The second use comes into play when you recognize that you've hurt someone, or done something wrong, or not taken care of someone, and you not only feel bad but also realize that you need forgiveness—forgiveness from God and, quite often, forgiveness from the person you hurt.

The two sets of relationships again. Okay, I see what you mean. But that raises another question for me, because I think a lot of people have a bad impression of church precisely because it seems to be all about guilt and shame and making people feel bad.

That's an important point. I want to be very clear that there's a difference between guilt and shame. Guilt is feeling bad about something you've *done*. Shame is feeling bad about who you *are*. I realize we sometimes say, "I feel ashamed" and more or less mean "I feel guilty," but there is a difference. Guilt can be an appropriate response to some situations, as it means we're taking responsibility for something we've done and expressing our regret and sorrow. But shame is never helpful or healthy and is not something God wants for us. Keep in mind, the whole point of the Exodus story is about how much God loves God's people and gives the law as a gift, not to help them become God's people but because they already are.

Yeah, that's important to keep in mind. So the second use of the law doesn't only make you feel bad, it also creates this larger sense that we're not perfect, we make mistakes, we need forgiveness—apart from whether we feel bad about something in the moment. And in all these ways the law makes us aware of our need for God.

That's part of it. I mean, maybe you sometimes feel bad about speeding, maybe sometimes you don't. In the larger picture, the law in its second use reveals that there are a lot of ways—some small, others much larger—in which we don't live into God's intentions for us and need forgiveness and grace.

That makes sense.

I'd even go further and say that the primary goal of the second use of the law isn't to make you feel bad at all, even if guilt is sometimes an appropriate feeling, but instead is intended to make us more aware about reality.

Reality?

Yeah. Reality. In this sense, Luther compares the law to a mirror that never fails to tell the truth about us and therefore reflects who we are and the world we're in. And so the law in its second use reveals things like the fact that we're all mortal and will one day die. It reminds us that, even when we try not to, we sometimes hurt each other and ourselves. It shows us that, no matter how hard we try, we can't actually *not* sin.

Can you say more about that? It's not like I think I'm perfect or anything, but that seems like a really bold, all-encompassing statement.

It's meant to be. Think for a minute about the clothes we wear, the food we eat, the cars we drive, and basically the lives we enjoy. All of it comes at a price—and I don't mean just what we pay to buy things. There are all kinds of ways in which elements of our way of life may hurt the environment or even other people who are making our clothes or live with less because of our affluence. And even if we decide to live more simply or drive less or do all kinds of things to minimize these negative outcomes, there's no way to extricate ourselves from this world we're in.

You're right—that is pretty comprehensive! When you put it that way, I'm not sure there's a way out. I mean, it feels like the whole world is kind of broken.

And beautiful too. In the Genesis stories, God creates the world and calls it good, and it still is. But there are also stories about how humans not only make individual mistakes but are also caught up in a web of brokenness. Paul once wrote of the whole creation "groaning" under the weight of sin and in the hope of redemption (Romans 8:22).

That's an apt way of putting it. And all this is the work of the law in its second use?

Yes, the law in its second use makes us aware of the poignant, at times painful, reality of our beautiful but broken, precious but imperfect world.

And recognizing that makes us aware of our need for God.

For God's grace, for God's forgiveness, for God's goodness, for God's redemption, for God's love. All of which is made most clear in the story of Jesus. Luther describes the main purpose of the second use of the law not as making us feel guilty or even as revealing sin or reality but rather as "driving us to Christ." He believes that when you take an honest look around, you realize that we can't save ourselves and we need Jesus to do that.

So the second use of the law doesn't really end in itself?

What do you mean?

Well, with the first use, you pretty much get what you need right off the bat. "Don't steal." "Take care of each other." "Help your neighbor." That's clear and covers the bases. But the second use of the law pushes you toward something else—namely, God.

That's helpful. Yes, the second use isn't meant to work alone but instead is supposed to lead you to the gospel, the good news that, whether we'd expect it or not, God loves us more than we could imagine, and shows that love most clearly in the person of Jesus. In this sense, law and gospel work together to tell us the whole truth about our life in the world.

The *whole* truth? As in "the truth, the whole truth, and nothing but the truth"?

Pretty much. Essentially, the law in its second use tells us the truth about the world and about ourselves: that we fall short of God's expectations, that we fail to love each other and ourselves as we should, that we don't take care of the world God gave us as a gift, that the whole world, in fact, is caught in a web of brokenness. The gospel then tells us about God's loving response to us in Jesus. That's the good news—rather than punish us, God forgives us in love, and rather than abandon us, God comes to us in grace. So the gospel is the "second truth" about God's grace that responds to the "first truth" revealed by the law that our lives and the world are captive to sin.

"Sin." That's another one of those church words that isn't very popular and, maybe more importantly, probably turns people off because it feels like you're calling people bad.

I get it, but a few things in response. First, in the Bible "sin" doesn't so much name all the little things we've done wrong as it describes a force in the world that intends to rob the children of God of abundant life.

Really?

Whenever Paul writes about sin, for instance, it's not in the plural—"sins"—but in the singular—"sin"—this force that seeks to pull us away from God and pull the world apart. In this sense, and as Luther regularly writes, sin is the enemy—our enemy, God's enemy, the thing Jesus comes to defeat and to rescue us from. For Paul and Luther, sin essentially holds us hostage and prevents us from embracing the abundant life God wants for all of us.

That's really interesting and, to be honest, not what I expected.

I think this surprises a lot of people. My second point is that sin describes a condition or state we're caught up in. Naming the reality of sin isn't meant to create a sense of shame but to offer a realistic description of our situation so we recognize we cannot do this all alone. This, again, is what Luther means by saying the second use of the law "drives us to Christ."

Okay, that's making more and more sense.

Third, naming the reality of sin—or, more importantly, confessing our sin—can be really freeing. You can stop pretending, for starters.

Pretending?

Yeah, pretending you have it all together. Pretending you've never been hurt. Pretending you haven't hurt others. The truth is that we do things we regret, things that hurt others and the world and ourselves, things we wish we wouldn't have done. And I think it can be really freeing—and healthy—to confess that.

You know, it's kind of weird, but you're absolutely right. When I've done something to hurt someone, or been hurt by someone else, it's like that thing—what you're calling sin—had a stranglehold on me. It wasn't until I could apologize—which I hadn't thought of as confessing—or the other person apologized to me, that it was possible to move forward.

I agree, and that's also what is freeing about confession, as least when it's paired with forgiveness! It gives you a chance to move on, to not be stuck with something that happened in the past, to remember that the future is still open. In Paul's letter to the Colossians, he says that by forgiving us God essentially nailed the record of all our misdeeds to the cross (2:13-14). In this way, confession and forgiveness open up the future.

That's pretty incredible.

Well, you said it yourself. Sin, whether it's what you've done or what someone has done to you, can get a stranglehold on you and make it feel like it's the only reality there is. Forgiveness breaks that. In fact, I'd say forgiveness not only opens up the future but creates the possibility of a new one.

Forgiveness creates a new future? Say more about that.

Sure. By and large, we live in a cause-and-effect world. You do something that causes something else to happen, and so forth. That assumption is pretty much the basis for all our attempts to understand the natural world through science.

"For every action, there is an equal and opposite reaction": Newton's third law of motion.

Yes, that gets at it. Newton, of course, is talking about physics and trying to understand the interaction of force, mass, and so on. But you're right that there's a similar law of cause and effect across our human experience. Ralph Waldo Emerson called it the "law of laws" because it explains pretty much everything that exists in terms of some prior cause. And in the social realm of human relationships, forgiveness interrupts this and creates another possibility.

Okay, I see where you're going. This is very much like what we talked about earlier. Instead of buying into "an eye for an eye and a tooth for a tooth," Jesus says, "Turn the other cheek." And that's not, I gather, meant to encourage anyone to keep getting beat up but instead is a metaphor for forgiveness, for interrupting the law of cause and effect we're talking about.

Exactly, and this is really important and worth slowing down to make sure we understand.

Sounds good.

It's interesting that the Bible names this cause-and-effect dimension of human experience that we're talking about. In his letter to the Galatians, Paul writes, "you reap whatever you sow" (6:7), which builds on all kinds of stories and sayings in the Old Testament as well.

You reap what you sow. Yeah, that pretty much sums up cause and effect.

But rather than assume that cause and effect is the only law at work, the Bible invites us to see how forgiveness interrupts that cause and effect, even breaks the cycle to create a new possibility. And that is, indeed, what Jesus means by "turning the other cheek." It's definitely not an excuse for abuse. In fact, it assumes the person in question has a choice and, therefore, some power.

So, it's like Jesus is saying, "I know you could hit the person back. But slow down and think. You have options. Don't buy into the idea that your only choice is revenge."

Exactly.

What an incredibly timely conviction. I mean, there is so much violence and fear these days. Sometimes it feels like we're caught up in a spiral of retaliation. It sounds like Luther, following Jesus, is trying to challenge that assumption and break the cause-and-effect cycle.

Martin Luther King Jr. also tried to do that. In his book *The Strength to Love* he wrote, "Returning hate for hate multiplies hate, adding deeper darkness to a night already devoid of stars. Darkness cannot drive out darkness, only light can do that. Hate cannot drive out hate, only love can do that."[1]

Okay, I see what you mean about forgiveness creating a new future. Interestingly, though, King talks about love.

That is interesting, and important. Forgiveness stems from God's great love for us, of course, but it also reminds us that the gospel— because that's what we've been talking about—isn't limited to forgiveness but instead is whatever loving way God responds to the reality that is limiting or oppressing us.

I think I'm following, but could you say more?

Absolutely. First off, do you remember when we talked about the uses of the law?

Sure. The law isn't static, it does things. Like restraining us from hurting each other and encouraging us to help each other in its first use, and revealing our need for grace in its second use.

Yes, the different uses of the law describe its distinct actions or functions. Well, the gospel is the same. It *does* something. It sets something in motion. It functions in a certain way to make something happen.

Like forgiveness creating a new possibility, instead of the constant cycle of cause-and-effect retaliation.

Exactly.

Okay, so the gospel also is about doing something. Didn't you say earlier that the law—at least in its second use—and the gospel go together, that the law leads to the gospel?

Right. We talked about the way the law in its second use functions, or does something to us, and the particular thing the law may do to us, in turn, shapes how the gospel functions.

Hmm. Maybe this would be a good time for an example or two?

Good idea. We've been talking mainly about forgiveness, but earlier we also said that sin doesn't only name the things we've done wrong but also names this larger force that seeks to rob us of abundant life.

I remember.

Which means that if you say, for instance, "I'm sorry for what I said to you," it makes sense for me to say, "I forgive you."

Definitely.

But if you're not talking about something you've done wrong but rather talking about something related more to the brokenness of the world, for instance, that someone you cared about has died from cancer, then another response might be more appropriate.

Because if I say, "I'm really sad because my friend just died from cancer," and you say, "You're forgiven," that would sound pretty weird, even kind of insensitive.

Exactly. In that case, I might say, "I'm sorry you're sad. Because of Jesus' death on the cross, God knows what it is like to suffer loss and is with you." Or maybe, "I'm sorry for your loss. In Jesus' resurrection, we have the promise that Jesus triumphed over death, and so your loved one will also be raised to new life."

So, depending on how the law functions, the gospel may function differently too.

Yes. If the problem is fear, the gospel response may be courage. If it's despair, hope; meaninglessness, meaning; and so on.

Got it. It's kind of the two truths again. The law names our condition (first truth), the gospel responds to it (second truth). So whatever need or problem we're naming in the law, the gospel responds appropriately. But behind the variety of gospel responses, it's still always God's gracious response to us and our condition. So, again, it seems like in all of this, law and gospel go together.

That's an important observation. If you only hear the law and its relentless description of reality, it's hard not to end up in despair. But if you only hear the gospel, it's kind of hard to believe it, or at least believe it's addressed to you.

I'm not sure I'm following that last part about believing the gospel is addressed to you.

Think about when you are first getting to know someone whom you like and who you hope will like you in return. Most of us experience something of a dilemma in this situation. On the one hand, we may be a bit cautious about showing our real selves fully and letting that person really get to know us right away, because we don't want to risk rejection—I mean, that's happened to all of us at one time or another, and it's no fun! On the other hand, we also know deep down that if someone doesn't know us, how can they genuinely love us? Maybe they just love the person we're pretending to be. Eventually, we reveal ourselves to those who are important to us, because we know that the only way to trust that you are fully loved is to be confident that you are fully known.

That's helpful. I totally agree that you have to trust that someone really knows you in order to believe that they really love you, but I'd never thought of that in terms of our relationship with God.

As we've seen at several points, Luther's theology is surprisingly relational, interested in the relationship we have with God—or, better yet, the relationship God has with us—and the relationships we have with each other. In this case, law and gospel work together so that we don't only hear about God's love but trust it.

Which means that before you will believe the "I love you" of the gospel you need to hear the "I know you" of the law.

That's a great way of putting it!

Thanks. What I find interesting is that Luther's theology is both relational, as we were just saying, and experiential. I mean, being known, being loved, these are experiences, not concepts. It feels like we are back to law and gospel not just *saying* things but really *doing* things—in this case, creating a relationship between you and God.

Right. We often talk about "law and gospel" as a theological shorthand for all of this. Luther is clear that he's interested in how the law and the gospel actually *function* in our lives. He sees this as the best way to describe how we experience God acting in our lives and in the world right now. That's why Luther uses a lot of verbs when talking about the function of the law and the gospel.

Verbs?

Yeah. For the law in its second use, Luther says the law "wounds" or "humbles" or even "destroys," because of the way it breaks down our defenses and pierces through both our pretending and our pride. He summarizes all this by saying the law "leads us to true knowledge of ourselves." In contrast, Luther says the gospel "heals," "gives life," "helps," "elevates," "honors," and ultimately "creates a new person."[2]

Luther is committed to what I would call a "present-tense" under-standing of God.

"Present-tense" view of God? Explain that.

Sure. It's easy for us to think that God only did things during Bible times—a long, long time ago. And it's also easy to think that what we do in church is pretty theoretical. But Luther feels both of those assumptions are dead wrong. He believes God is still at work, still active, still doing things in the present, not just the past. And the primary way Luther thinks God is active is in the word, in the proc-lamation of law and gospel.

The proclamation of law and gospel? That sounds like preaching.

Preaching is definitely important to Luther. But proclamation can also include naming these things in our lives, or reassuring each other of God's love and forgiveness, or even reminding each other that God is with us.

So we can all make use of law and gospel, not just the preacher.

Exactly. In fact, even though Luther values good preaching highly, he feels that the church of his day is getting in the way by saying only priests can offer forgiveness and grace. Luther instead follows what it says in the New Testament: that everyone is a priest. By virtue of being baptized and given the promise of God's love and forgive-ness, each one of us can share God's love and forgiveness with oth-ers (1 Peter 2:4–9).

So I'm a priest?

A priest is essentially someone who has been authorized to speak on behalf of God. And according to Luther, anyone who has experi-enced the consequences of sin or the brokenness of the world (sec-ond use of the law), which has led them to experience the life-giving quality of God's love (gospel), and is willing to share it with others is a priest.

I have to say I've never thought of it that way. Kinda cool, being a priest!

Yeah, it is. Especially when you realize this means each of us has an opportunity to introduce people to the God who is still at work freeing us to admit our need and then giving us the incredible gifts of grace, love, and forgiveness.

That is really cool.

And it even gets better.

How so?

Well, once you understand that God is still working in and through the law and the gospel out of love, you also get a sense of how Luther's theology of grace can shape our whole lives.

Seriously? I'd like to hear more about that. Maybe we can go there next.

Sounds like a great idea.

Insights and Questions

CHAPTER 4

The Ambidextrous God

*The Two Kingdoms and God's
Ongoing Work in the World*

Okay, so I know we're going to talk about how Luther's sense that God is
still working in the world can shape our whole lives, and I'm looking forward
to getting to that. But can I start with another question?

Of course.

I've been thinking about where we ended up last time. We talked about
how Luther's insight that we are justified by grace through faith, instead of
through works, introduces him to what feels like a whole other God—or at
least a very different picture of God than the one he grew up with. This God
of unconditional love wants only good things for us, gives us the law both
to help us take care of each other and to remind us that we need grace, and
gives us the gospel—the promise that no matter what we do or what happens
to us or where we go, God will never stop loving us.

That's an excellent summary. So what's your question?

Well, I guess it just seems too good to be true. I know we already said this
isn't what you would probably expect from looking at the natural world,
where it seems like the operative rule is "the survival of the fittest" and all

that, but this God is beyond surprising. I mean, unconditional love. Maybe, maybe if you're lucky, you've experienced something like that if you had really good parents or a very close friendship or a fantastic spouse. But even then, we still hurt each other from time to time. So, I feel weird and a bit guilty saying this, but why should we believe this? *How* can we believe it?

If it makes you feel any better, Luther feels the same way.

Really? Even after his breakthrough about justification by grace?

Yes, even after that and, in many ways, for the rest of his life, he still struggles to believe the gospel that changed his life. In fact, he writes at one point, "It is the hardest thing possible to be surely persuaded in our hearts that we have the forgiveness of sins and peace with God by grace alone."[1]

Yes! That is exactly how I feel. So what does he do about it?

I'll try to answer that in a few steps. First, let's go deeper into the question of why the gospel is hard to believe. Then we can explore what reason we have for believing it. And after that we can talk about what Luther does, and what we might do, to deal with what is, at least for Luther, a lifelong challenge.

Sounds good. So . . . why is the gospel hard to believe?

I'd say there are at least two reasons, and we've mentioned both in passing. First, we are by nature rather insecure. We saw that in the Adam and Eve story a while back. They had a hard time trusting God, and therefore had a hard time accepting the identity God offered them, so they were susceptible to the serpent's suggestion that they take matters into their own hands and establish their identities on their own.

Right. Original insecurity comes before original sin.

Good memory. And, to our point, we still struggle with that same insecurity, always wondering if we're good enough, or have done enough, or whether we deserve love and respect.

I don't know anyone who doesn't have those insecurities.

Interestingly, some theologians have suggested that this insecurity, or restlessness, ultimately leads us back to God.

How so?

Saint Augustine, whose work is very influential for Luther, opens his book *Confessions* by writing to God and saying, "our heart is restless until it rests in thee." And the seventeenth-century poet George Herbert, in his poem "The Pulley," describes God giving humanity all the gifts of creation except rest or contentment, so that we would always need to return to God for a sense of ultimate completion and peace.

That's interesting and again highlights the importance of our relationship with God. But, to be honest, it's also confusing. I mean, is insecurity what keeps us from believing God loves us or what draws us back to God?

I'd put it this way. Freedom demands a level of independence, but with that independence comes insecurity.

Why?

To be free is by definition to have choices—choices about actions, decisions, careers, relationships, ethical dilemmas, you name it. And as long as we have choices, we wonder and worry about which one is best. Sometimes it's easy to know, but certainly not always. Added to that, because we're free, we need to figure out who we are, what we value, and whether and how we have value. Hence, insecurity.

That's a lot of reasons to be insecure!

And that insecurity makes it hard to believe God fully loves us, but God also works through that same insecurity to draw us back to God. I'm not sure I agree with Herbert that God *made* us insecure; it's more that it is an unavoidable element of having a measure of freedom. Again, relationship is key. A good relationship requires a measure of independence but only works when the partners in the relationship also depend on each other. Does that make sense?

Yes, though it's a lot to think about! Maybe for now it's enough to recognize that our insecurity makes it hard to trust that someone completely and unconditionally loves and accepts you.

Fair enough. And what deepens that insecurity is what you mentioned a moment ago—our experience in the world is often not one of absolute acceptance and unconditional love. If we're fortunate, as you said, we have some people in our lives who have tried to do that, but none of us loves and accepts others perfectly, and so none of us has been loved and accepted perfectly.

That's also, I suppose, part of living in a broken world.

Right. And I think that's key. God's love comes into our world but also promises another one.

Another world?

Not another world in the sense of another planet somewhere out beyond our solar system but another world in the sense of another reality. Jesus names it "the kingdom of God," and he didn't mean another kingdom or country like ours but instead was naming a different *reality* that is no longer captive to sin and death and, for that matter, insecurity.

Interesting. Say more.

I often think that artists sometimes do a better job of capturing these kinds of realities than theologians, so let me reference Shakespeare's *King Lear*, which some think is the greatest piece of literature in the English language.

Okay, but, just to let you know, I haven't read *King Lear*—or even the *CliffsNotes*®—since eleventh-grade English class, so you'll need to refresh me on some of the details.

No problem. And I'll keep it brief. Essentially, Lear is a king of England ages ago. At the beginning of the play, he's getting ready to retire. As we find out, Lear is both insecure and controlling, which often seem to go together! So he's got everything planned out: he's going to divide his kingdom into three parts, one for each of his daughters, and then have each one tell him how much she loves him and assign portions of the kingdom accordingly. The best speech gets the best part of the kingdom, and so on.

Wait a second. He's going to have them make speeches about their love for him and then reward them for that? I have to say, that seems not just insecure but incredibly superficial.

No question. And that's what his youngest daughter thinks as well. Her name is Cordelia, and she's Lear's favorite. He plans on giving her the best part of the kingdom and retiring to live with her. But she messes up his plans when she refuses to say anything, because she knows the whole thing is bogus and, as you said, superficial.

What does Lear do?

He's so mad that she's screwed up his plans that he banishes her to France and divides England into two parts, which he gives to his two older daughters.

How does that work out?

Not well! In fact, most of the rest of the play describes the consequences of Lear's superficial understanding of love, as he is rejected by first one daughter and then the other, until he finds himself all but abandoned and going slightly mad. Until, that is, Cordelia comes back.

Then what happens?

Well, Lear is pretty sure she's there to punish him. And, oddly, that's okay with him. Or at least he understands it. He lives, after all, in an "eye-for-an-eye" kind of world. And he figures that if the world is just and he gets punished for his sins, at least he can look forward to the punishment of his enemies, because he believes he is, as he says at one point, "a man more sinned against than sinning."

Kind of bleak.

Or realistic, depending on how you look at it.

True. After all, this is pretty much the world we imagined you could figure out on your own just by looking at nature. The world of rewards and punishments and all the rest.

Exactly. And that's what makes the scene with Lear and Cordelia amazing. It begins when Lear, still half-mad, recognizes that it really is Cordelia. As I said, he assumes she's there to punish him. After all, that's what he would do in her place. So he says, "If you have poison, I will drink it," lamenting, "for I know you do not love me. Your sisters have, as I remember, done me some wrong. You have some cause. They have not." To which Cordelia responds, "No cause, no cause," offering a measure of forgiveness Lear did not think possible.

Wow, that's pretty moving. And what does Lear do in response?

That's the part I find so interesting . . . and true. Because all Lear can manage in response to Cordelia's forgiveness and love is to ask, "Am I in France?"

What?

Confusing, I know. His servants think he's still crazy, so they reply, "In your own kingdom, sir." But I think Lear's madness has left him, replaced by a sense of grace that makes him feel like he's been ushered into a whole other world. And to be honest, I think that, in a very real sense, Lear *has* left his world—left behind the moral geography of an England dominated by justice rather than love that, while it may create a modicum of order, also breeds the madness that comes from our relentless, remorseless tracking of every slight or injury. Lear's left all that behind because, for the first time in his life, he has experienced unconditional love.

And he has a hard time believing it. So it feels like he's in France. I totally get that. So, what do we do about the struggle to believe the gospel?

Well, first, let's tackle the question of why we should believe it in the first place. In Shakespeare's play, Lear comes to believe—and to be transformed by his belief—because Cordelia actually comes back for him. Not only that, but when Lear is captured, Cordelia stays with him, sacrificing everything she has for him.

Beautiful, but also sad.

Well, it is a tragedy. And, interestingly, it's set in a pre-Christian England, so perhaps for Shakespeare it can only end up as a tragedy.

What do you mean?

I think Shakespeare is not only an amazing playwright but, like a lot of artists, also a pretty good theologian in that he sees the truth of things. And so Cordelia embodies the grace of Christ that Shakespeare has experienced through his life in the church. But all this happens before the gospel has come to England, so Cordelia and her sacrificial love foreshadow what will come in Christ, but don't fully embody it.

Maybe Shakespeare is pointing out that we can only get so far on our own apart from God, that even our own attempts at perfect love come up short.

That's an interesting possibility. If so, it would push us to go back to another story, the gospel story of Jesus' sacrificial love embodied on the cross.

Which, for Luther, is the proof of how much God loves us.

Right, even if, and maybe especially when, it's an absurd truth that no one expects. What's key is that, even though Jesus dies on the cross, the story doesn't end in tragedy, because it doesn't stop there. The resurrection of Jesus shows that God's love is stronger than our sin and fear and insecurity and even death.

So the cross shows us the depth of God's love, and the resurrection shows us that God's love conquers all.

Right. And that brings us to what we can do about the struggle to believe all of this.

Great. I've been wondering.

It's really pretty simple: we can go to church.

Seriously? I have to say that I was looking for more.

I get it. Church doesn't sound all that exciting to everyone.

And that's on a good day!

I understand. Sometimes what we do at church can seem routine, even predictable. And, to be honest, that's what a lot of folks like about it. In the middle of a crazy and constantly changing world, there's something familiar to come back to.

I get that. Though sometimes I wouldn't mind changing things up a bit.

And I get that as well. So here's the thing. Churches have lots of freedom to think about how they put together a worship service—traditional, contemporary, something in between. What matters is that they're clear about one thing.

Which is . . . ?

That at the heart of the service are the opportunity and necessity to tell us once again that God loves us—unconditionally and forever—no matter what. Because, to tell you the truth, I think it's really hard to believe that message for more than about seven days in a row.

Say more.

Sure. At church, the music, readings, liturgy, and sermon should all work together to say clearly and loudly that the God who created and still sustains the vast cosmos also knows that you exist, and cares deeply and passionately about you—about your ups and downs, your hopes and frustrations, your dreams and disappointments. And, even more, this God is committed to going with you and staying with you and holding onto you through everything that happens in this life—even through death—and into new life.

Okay, that makes a lot of sense. And when you put it that way, we're right back to where we started: this is incredibly good news, so good it's hard to believe.

Exactly. And when everything comes together in worship you hear this promise and believe it and go out filled with confidence that God loves you and is with you. Then you go back into your everyday life of routines and appointments and deadlines and disappointments and, by the time Friday rolls around . . .

Or some weeks by Tuesday morning!

Right. Before long, you just . . .

. . . Have a hard time believing again. I get it.

And so you come back to church, the one place where you can expect
to hear this message of unconditional grace and love.

**I have to say, that does make church sound more interesting. I mean, if I
could count on the fact that, no matter what's going on in my life or what
happened in the past week, I could come to worship and hear that God loves
me, that God sees worth in me, that God forgives me and goes with me in all
of life . . . well, that would be worth getting up for.**

And that, at its best, is what church should be—the means by which
we hear again and again the incredible promise that God loves us,
forgives us, and goes with us. And though some folks think of the
church as a super-quiet place, Luther once described it as a "mouth
house," a place where people are always talking about God's mercy
and love.

**Awesome. Thanks for taking the detour. I'm glad to know I'm not the only
one who struggles to believe this good news, and also that there's something
I can do about it. Now let's go back to how believing in God's love and that
God is still at work in the world can shape your whole life.**

Actually, we don't really have to "go back" to anything. We're already
here.

What do you mean?

Just that being reminded of God's love for you doesn't just help you
believe. It also helps you go out into the world to see where God is
already at work and to partner with God to care for the world God
loves so much.

Okay, you've gotten ahead of me. God's already out in the world and at work?

Yup.

Where?

Where not?

Uh . . . you're going to need to give me more to work with.

No problem. Let's go back to the whole law–gospel thing.

Okay.

So we talked about the first use of the law . . .

Yes, it's God's gift that both helps us take care of each other and keeps us in check when we're, well, not in the mood to do that.

And the second use?

Points out our need for grace and . . . drives us to Christ. At least I think that's the way Luther put it.

Exactly. Which means, as we've already said, that the law, in its second use, and the gospel go together.

Definitely. Law without gospel drives you to despair, but gospel without law is hard to trust.

Right.

Or, to put it in the language we used, the "I know you" of the law without the "I love you" of the gospel leaves us with no hope. But without the "I know you" of the law, it's pretty hard to trust God's "I love you."

Nice. And all this is another great example of how Luther's theology, when you get right down to it, is very relational, as it focuses both on our relationship with God and . . .

Our relationships with each other.

And that holds true for how God is at work in the world.

I was with you right up to that point.

We started with church. That's where you hear how the second use of the law and the gospel work together to let you know that God knows you and loves you and will go with you throughout your life.

Got it.

So God is *at work* in church helping you hear and believe the good news that God is on your side, totally for you and with you.

Okay, that makes sense. But what about in the rest of the world outside of church?

If the law, in its second use, and the gospel describe how God is at work in the *church*, it's the law, now in its first use, that describes how God is working in the *world*. Think again about what the first use of the law does.

The law encourages us to take care of our neighbor and keeps us in check when we don't feel like it.

And how does the law do that?

You know, that seems like it should be a pretty easy answer, but I'm not sure. I mean, I guess it helps to know about the ten commandments. But, honestly, while I'm sure learning about the ten commandments in Sunday school or posting them somewhere is a start, if that's all you're going to do, it seems a little weak.

What do you mean?

Just that knowing we should care for our neighbor doesn't mean we do. Or even that we know how. And it doesn't necessarily make it possible to do it, especially when you realize how many people need help. So now let me put the question back to you. How does the first use of the law actually do its work, beyond being a posted on a wall?

Luther's answer is actually pretty simple, but it also might surprise you.

I'm getting used to this.

Actually, it's a two-part answer. The first part is that God takes care of us through institutions.

Say again?

I know, I know, institutions get a bad rap these days. But Luther believes God set up institutions to help us take care of each other. Think, for a minute, about hospitals.

Ah, I see what you mean. Hospitals help lots of people.

And what about schools?

Yeah, schools do too.

And the police and fire departments?

I see where you're going. So God is at work through all these different agencies that do first-use-of-the-law kinds of things like taking care of people, educating people, and protecting people. And when you put it that way, the number of institutions and agencies and all the rest that God can use is nearly endless.

Definitely. The Red Cross. Habitat for Humanity. Lutheran World Relief. Homeless shelters. Counseling centers. Domestic-violence shelters. After-school programs. Food banks. Job-retraining programs. Veterans' programs. The list could go on and on.

Which is really good, because there are tons and tons of people who need help in some way. But it does get hard to keep track of.

Luther actually divides all the different ways that God does . . . what did you call it?

First-use-of-the-law kinds of things.

Right. Luther divides all the different ways God does first-use-of-the-law kinds of things into two main institutions. The first is the family.

Interesting. I didn't see that coming.

Well, for Luther family is the first and most basic community that is pretty much entirely set up to make sure we get taken care of. Babies come into this world utterly vulnerable, so without a family their chances of surviving, let alone flourishing, would be bleak.

That makes sense. And the second institution.

The government.

Okay, I didn't see that one coming either.

Police and fire departments protect us, help us, and keep us from hurting each other—all first-use-of-the-law kinds of things—and they're part of government. And so are most of the schools that educate our kids and prepare them for productive lives—again, a major first-use-of-the-law kind of thing. And there are lots of other agencies organized or set up by the government that help people when they're struggling.

I see what you mean.

The government also makes laws that are supposed to protect us. In fact, the *primary* thing governments are supposed to do is create conditions for civilized and peaceful life.

Which is totally a first-use-of-the-law kind of thing.

Do you remember when we mentioned Thomas Hobbes, the seventeenth-century philosopher?

The optimistic fellow who said life is "nasty, brutish, and short"?

That's the one. Well, he rendered that less-than-optimistic, but probably fairly accurate assessment of the natural world when he was arguing for the importance of government, which he described as a social contract people made with one another to keep the peace and promote civilization.

Reminds me of the Preamble to the U.S. Constitution:

> *We the People of the United States, in Order to form a more perfect Union, establish Justice, insure domestic Tranquility, provide for the common defence, promote the general Welfare, and secure the Blessings of Liberty to ourselves and our Posterity, do ordain and establish this Constitution for the United States of America.*

I'm impressed. You've got it memorized.

Credit my eighth-grade civics teacher.

There you go. Teachers make a difference!

Definitely.

In any event, Hobbes's political theory was certainly part of what shaped the U.S. Constitution, which is, of course, the foundational document of our government. And, as it turns out, the Constitution begins with all these first-use-of-the-law kinds of things like establishing justice and so on.

All very interesting and helpful. At the same time, it feels like you risk oversimplifying by lumping all those different agencies under the category of "government."

There's no question that there are many, many more institutions today than in Luther's time. But even today, most of the institutions we named wouldn't be able to exist without the overarching society set up and maintained by having an orderly government.

Yeah, I see what you mean. I think I'm still mulling over why, of all the institutions we talked about and all the ways people try to take care of each other, Luther focuses on government and the family.

Actually, Luther sees those two as being similar.

How so?

Well, the family keeps the peace, promotes order, and makes it possible for people to thrive in what we might call the private arena of the home, while government does the same in the public arena of our civic life together. In this sense, government functions like your parents, just writ large. This is why Luther derives the authority of government from the commandment to honor your father and mother. Government, because it is authorized by God to create safe societies, should be honored as parents should be honored.

Okay, but that raises a *really* big question.

Yes?

What happens when government doesn't do what it's supposed to do? I mean, yeah, sure, government is supposed to keep us safe, and create the conditions for civilization, and establish justice and domestic tranquility and all the rest. But sometimes it doesn't. Sometimes it doesn't seem to work well at all. Sometimes it feels like there's all this partisan bickering and not much gets done. And sometimes it's corrupt. And then, in some countries at different times, it's really, really corrupt, and it's hard to believe it's authorized by God at all. Given this, are we supposed to honor government at all times, even when it's not doing what it's supposed to do?

That is a big question, and a really important one. So I want to try to answer it in a couple ways.

Okay.

The first is to acknowledge that Luther does indeed have a pretty high view of government or what he might call authorized, legal rule. And he lives and writes during the Middle Ages, when the mortality rate was very high due to war, plagues, and so on. Many people didn't live to old age. This gives Luther a healthy respect for the necessity of law and order.

It sounds a lot like the "nasty, brutish, and short" part of life we talked about.

Exactly, particularly as Luther is writing a century before Hobbes is born. Like Hobbes, he thinks the social contract of government is incredibly important and, in this sense, a gift from God.

That makes sense but doesn't quite answer the question of how bad government has to be before you stop honoring it.

No, it doesn't. And, frankly, Luther may have struggled to answer the question to our satisfaction. He feels that even a bad government is better than no government, because when there's absolutely no government, chaos and anarchy reign. When that happens, the most vulnerable usually suffer the worst.

Like in the French Revolution?

Definitely. Or, for that matter, more recently. Think about war-torn countries in our day, with huge regions where there is no effective government. Chaos reigns, driving people from their homeland to take thousand-mile journeys as refugees, just for a chance to survive. Or consider when a government, even if it's a really corrupt government, falls, only to be replaced by warlords or ethnic factions, and everything is even worse. Here's the thing: human beings seem to have this nasty penchant for killing each other for all kinds of reasons, and Luther tends to think even a bad government does a better job of preventing that kind of savagery than no government at all.

Okay, I see what he means. But are there ever times when you just give up on government? I mean, what about during World War II and the Nazi government in Germany? Was that really better than no government?

Your question is spot-on and points out the potential weaknesses of Luther's theology in this area, or at least a weakness in the way people understood it.

Hmm. I'm not sure I'm following. Can you say more?

Sure. Germany, not surprisingly, has long had a lot of Lutherans. And some people think that one of the reasons the Nazis were able to do so much damage was that Germans, and especially German Lutherans, were too eager to give authority to government, any government, even a government as evil as the Nazi one.

Was that Luther's theology, or the way it was understood?

I'd say a bit of both, but mostly the latter. In terms of Luther's theology, we've already said that he had a really, really hard time imagining a situation where it was better to have no government or to try to overthrow a government than have a bad government. But as governments have evolved, and as technology and weaponry become more advanced—giving government more lethal power—it's harder to make that case.

And that's what we see in Nazi Germany, a bad government with the technology to kill millions.

Right. But this weakness or limitation already shows up in Luther's lifetime.

How so?

Early in the Reformation, some groups of peasants, farmers, and laborers protest their treatment by the princes and magistrates, and they write to Luther for help.

Why did they write to Luther?

He'd become immensely popular because his theology of grace was really appealing to people who felt under the thumb of the church and, just as much, because people saw him stand up to the most powerful institution of his day and more or less win. So people saw Luther as a champion of the common person.

What does Luther do?

Well, at first, he writes the various princes and magistrates and tells them to shape up. He feels that a lot of the peasants' and laborers' complaints are totally fair. Keep in mind that Luther thinks the role of government is a parental role, to take care of the people the way parents take care of their children. And that clearly isn't happening, so Luther tells the princes and magistrates they aren't doing the job God gave them and to get with it. And he urges all sides to keep the peace.

Sounds like there's more to this story.

Unfortunately, there is. Two things happen. First, the princes more or less ignore Luther. I mean, what do they care about what this theologian says? Second, the peasants get tired of waiting for things to get better. They begin to take matters into their own hands, and things get violent. When Luther tries to meet with them and calm things down, they get pretty angry, spit on him, and threaten him.

Then what happens?

Luther gets really mad. He had, in fact, a pretty wicked temper that sometimes got the best of him and led him into serious trouble. In addition, from his medieval vantage point, he begins to worry that the peasants will overthrow the government and become a lawless mob, and then everything will go to hell in a handbasket. So partly from this fear, and partly out of his anger, he tells the princes that they must put down this unruly mob, using whatever force is necessary.

Yikes!

No kidding. At one point, he says the princes and magistrates should "stab, smite, and slay them." And they do. Truth be told, they were already doing that, but Luther's treatise on this subject—named, ominously, "Against the Robbing and Murdering Hordes of Peasants"[2]—gives them justification and leads to a terrible result. By the time it was done, the "Peasants' War," as it was later called, leads to the death of more than 100,000 people.

That's horrific!

Yes. And whatever the precise causes of the princes' actions, Luther shares some of the blame for his incendiary rhetoric that helped justify this tragedy. Beyond that, Luther's writings about the peasants illumine painfully the limitations of both Luther's theology and how it was applied.

It seems like one limitation is that he seriously underestimates the balance of power between a government and its people. It's already true in the Middle Ages, and becomes even more true as technology advances.

Right. In medieval times people were usually born into positions of authority, were not accountable to an electorate, as most rulers are today, and held much more power than the people they governed.

And what about the way Luther's theology is applied in this case?

Well, I'd argue that both Luther and the peasants fall short in applying it. The peasants take the law into their own hands, justifying their acts of violence by saying, essentially, that the end justifies the means.

What should they have done?

I think Luther would have said it was fine, indeed right, for them to protest, but not to do violence. Instead, they should have protested and suffered the consequences.

Easy for him to say.

Of course, but that doesn't mean he isn't willing to do the same. Once, when he heard that a farmer whose family was starving was imprisoned by his prince for stealing, Luther told the prince that it was his fault the farmer had to steal in the first place—he should be taking better care of the people. Luther went on to say that if the prince didn't release the farmer, Luther would start stealing to feed the farmer's family. Then the prince could put Luther in jail too.

What did the prince do?

He let the farmer go and gave him a job.

Okay, so I see what you mean. But it still seems really, really hard to suffer injustice without doing anything.

Ah, but you are doing something. By your suffering, you call attention to the injustice and separate yourself from those who are unjust by not acting like them and taking the law into your own hands. In both of these ways, you're more or less publicly shaming the unjust ruler and creating incentives to improve.

Like Luther does with the prince?

Right. And what Gandhi did with the British in India and what Martin Luther King Jr. did in the United States in relation to civil rights for African Americans.

Interesting. I hadn't made that connection. So protesting and suffering can be effective, even powerful, though they are really hard to pull off.

Very, very hard sometimes. And that brings me to Luther's failure. In my opinion, he gives up too quickly on his ability to persuade the princes.

What do you mean?

I said earlier that the princes ignored Luther. So Luther should have organized more leaders. And if he didn't find them in the princes, he should have looked to the church.

The church?

Yeah. It's one thing for Luther, who is fairly famous at this time, to protest and not be heard. It would be another thing if all the local priests and clergy and churches protested. That, indeed, would be hard to ignore.

Interesting, but it feels like a blurring of the separation of church and state. Or is that not a concern in the Middle Ages?

I assume you're referring to the first article of the U.S. Bill of Rights?

Yes. "Congress shall make no law respecting an establishment of religion, or prohibiting the free exercise thereof."

Wow, you really did have a great civics teacher!

Yup. And while I'm thinking of the First Amendment, I'm also thinking of Thomas Jefferson's later description of the impact of "building a wall of separation between Church and State." Your suggestion that Luther should have engaged the churches to protest the abuses of the princes could risk blurring that important distinction. But, again, maybe that wasn't a concern in Luther's day.

I'm glad you brought this up, and a couple of things in response. First, James Madison, the primary author of the Constitution and the Bill of Rights, actually credited Martin Luther as an influence, particularly with regard to the First Amendment.

I didn't learn that in civics class.

Madison said that in helping distinguish between how God works through the church and through the government, "the genius and courage of Luther led the way."[3]

Interesting.

Most often, Luther's beliefs about the respective roles of the church and government are described as his theory of "the two kingdoms."

"Kingdoms," like the "kingdom of God" that Jesus preached?

Not really, which is why I think "two kingdoms" isn't the best name for Luther's thought. "Kingdoms" sound like places, but what Luther is talking about is two different ways of working in the world. Some folks have suggested that two "governments," or two "kinds of rule" give this a more active sense. But since we already said God works through government, I think that can get confusing too. So I like to talk about God's "two hands."

Two hands?

Yeah. We do a whole lot of our work with our hands, and Luther's focus is on how God goes about the work of taking care of us, protecting us, blessing us, and saving us.

We've already been talking about that, haven't we? I mean, at church God works through the second use of the law and the gospel to promise God's love, acceptance, forgiveness, and presence with us. And in the first use of the law— particularly through the family and government—God helps us take care of each other, and restrains us when we only want to look out for ourselves.

That's right. And there you've named Luther's two kingdoms or, as I said, what I prefer to call God's two hands. Talking about "hands" makes it easier to distinguish between the different but related kinds of work God does. This will help us figure out how church and state might relate, and address the question of when we don't have to obey a government.

I'm all ears.

Okay, so to get at all this we need to go back to a tradition that Luther inherits and adapts, which started a thousand years or so before him.

That's a long time ago!

It is, which gives you a sense that you're not alone in these questions and that Christians have been thinking about all this for quite some time.

That's good to know. So what tradition did Luther inherit?

Basically, from at least the time of Saint Augustine, who lived between 354 and 430 CE, Christians had been describing God's work through the church with the adjective "right."

As in right versus wrong?

No, as in right versus left.

Kind of weird. But okay.

Actually, it's not as weird as it sounds. In the ancient world, there was a long-standing tradition that saw right as superior to left. The place of honor at a banquet, for instance, is to sit at the right hand of the host.

That sounds familiar.

You might be thinking of the Apostles' Creed. We confess about Jesus that "On the third day he rose again, he ascended into heaven, he is seated at the right hand of the Father," which is a reference to Acts 2:33.

I probably should have been thinking about that. But I was reminded of a line from the song "A Winter's Ball," from the Broadway musical *Hamilton*. In the previous song, we hear that Alexander Hamilton becomes Washington's "right-hand man." Then in this song, Aaron Burr, who doesn't like Hamilton all that much, wonders how such a "bother" as Hamilton gets "seated at the right hand of the father," referring to Washington.

Those are great examples. Exactly, to be a "right-hand man" is to be indispensable. And to sit at someone's "right hand" is a place of distinction, even intimacy, and to have access to that person and his or her authority. And, interestingly, traces of that past still linger. Take, for instance, two words in English: first, "gauche."

As in not cool, not in style, or socially awkward?

That's the one, and it's the French word for—you guessed it—"left."

Interesting.

And then there's "sinister."

As in really bad, even evil?

Right. Which is Latin for . . .

Let me guess: "left."

Right. Or, I should probably say, "correct"!

Very interesting and, again, a little weird that these distinctions have so much life. So, if the church is God's right hand, then I'm guessing the state—or as we've been talking about it, family and the government—is God's left hand?

Correct again.

So the state is inferior to the church?

For most of history, that's what theologians and church leaders have argued.

Which is in their self-interest, don't you think?

Absolutely. And for a lot of that time, rulers more or less agreed, especially if they claimed their office by "divine right."

"Divine right"?

Yes. Kings would claim that they were in positions of power—as opposed to someone else—because God had put them there. To make that claim stronger, they needed the support of the church and the pope. In return, the emperor supported the pope as the chief leader and interpreter of all things religious.

Sounds too comfy-cozy for me. I mean, couldn't that be dangerous?

Absolutely, and Luther pretty much agrees with you.

Really?

Yeah. Luther inherits the left–right terminology, but he goes against more than a thousand years of tradition by saying that the two kingdoms, governments, or as I prefer, hands are essentially equal. That is, because God works through both, both should be respected as important arenas or places where God does God's work.

So Luther doesn't think the church is superior to the state?

Nope. The difference for Luther isn't so much about superiority as it is clarity.

Clarity?

Right. Luther thinks it's easiest to see God at work in the proclamation of the gospel, in the baptism of a child, in the announcement of God's forgiveness, and in the promise that God will always be with us. At the same time, while we confess that God is at work through families and agencies and the government and all the rest, it can also be, as you've already pointed out, harder to detect God at work.

Ah, I see what you mean. Even good governments can be slow to get important work done, and even in the best of families there is still pain and disappointment.

Exactly. It's just not as easy to see God at work. For example, on the one hand, probably the best health care in the world is in the United States. Yet every time you go to file a claim, you know there are things that could be better. And, more importantly, too many people are left out. So God is at work through health care . . .

. . . But precisely because it's an institution run by people, it is harder to see God at work than when you're baptizing a baby or promising God's grace.

Exactly.

Okay, so I'm with you on God's two hands. The right is the church and its ministry of, for lack of a better word, grace. And the left is the family and

government and its work of promoting civil life. And according to Luther these two hands, while differing in how easy it is to perceive God in them, are nevertheless equally important to keeping the world running.

Right. In this sense, I like to say that God is "ambidextrous," and uses each hand as well as the other.

Nice. But I'm still not sure how this relates to what you said about Luther and how he should have enlisted other clergy to criticize the rulers of his day. Like I said, isn't that a blurring of the separation of church and state, a sort of hole in Jefferson's wall?

I'd say the key point is that it's Jefferson's wall—not Madison's, and not Luther's. What I mean is that while I think Luther would have affirmed Jefferson's basic sense of a separation between the powers and spheres of influence between the church (right hand) and state (left hand), he probably would have been more comfortable with a distinction rather than a "wall of separation."

Say some more.

Luther thinks that the two hands of God—like our own hands—work best in a kind of interdependent independence.

Interdependent independence? That's a mouthful.

Yeah, let me try to break it down. On the one hand, Luther thinks left and right each have their own independent work, sphere of influence, and authority. So he thinks government should not be making rules about religion, and religion should not act like government. When either happens, things begin to fall apart.

Which sounds a lot like what Madison's saying in the Bill of Rights.

Yes. But while they have their own independent authority and arenas, left and right also can support each other. Government creates a level of civic peace and stability that protects the freedom to exercise your faith, while religious leaders remind people that government is authorized by God to promote peace and good order. That's what I mean by interdependent independence. They each have their job to do but work best when they support each other.

That makes sense, but it also sounds a lot like the prior and probably too-cozy relationship between church and state we talked about.

Except that Luther thinks both hands have a role in not only supporting each other but also correcting each other. So if the church begins to exceed its role, say by opening up banks or trying to run some part of our civil life, then the job of the government is to tell the church to back off. And, similarly, when the government isn't doing its job to protect its people, the church should protest and tell it to get back to work.

Like Luther did with his prince.

Right. And this doesn't have to be a solitary affair. I've wondered what might have happened if the whole church had gotten involved in protesting the treatment of the peasants. No one knows, but if Luther had been more patient and more strategic and had more confidence in his own theology, or if the peasants had felt more support and didn't try to get their aims across by violence, maybe it would have been different.

But what if it wasn't? That is, what if the church leaders had protested vigorously and the peasants had waited patiently, and the princes still didn't care?

Actually, we don't have to imagine that, because that's what happens, as you mentioned earlier, during Nazi Germany.

Say more about that.

When the Nazis come to power, the church doesn't unify in opposition. Some church leaders join what is called the "German Christians" (*Deutsche Christen*), which is basically set up to support the extreme nationalism and outright prejudice of the Nazis and to take control of church practices. Not long after that, other church leaders, appalled by what's going on, form the "Confessing Church" (*Bekennende Kirche*) to protest this. One of the first things they do is offer a statement of faith called the Barmen Declaration—because it's written at a gathering in Barmen, Germany—that declares their opposition to anyone claiming authority to tell the church what it can preach, teach, or, for that matter, protest.

So they protest.

Yes. And work against the Nazis by defending Jews and by smuggling them out of Germany when things get worse. And for this, they also suffer, offering that as a witness to the crimes of the state.

But I gather none of this has any influence on the Nazis.

Right. Eventually some members of the Confessing Church, including the young Lutheran theologian Dietrich Bonhoeffer, decide that to be faithful to the gospel, and for that matter to Luther's sense of God's two hands, they must work for the downfall of the government. Bonhoeffer eventually is imprisoned for this work, then executed.

That's a really powerful story. I can't imagine that was an easy place to get to for Bonhoeffer.

Definitely not. Like Luther, he had a strong sense of the importance of authority, but there is a time and place when even a government crosses the line and not only does not do what God intends but insists on doing what God forbids. That's a tough call to make, and not to be made lightly, but Bonhoeffer and his colleagues felt that, based on their faith, they could not ignore what their government was doing.

That's interesting, and an important example of how the church can fulfill its role not simply to support government but also critique and at times resist it.

And it's not just overseas that churches protest against their government. That happens in the U.S. as well. Churches were in the forefront of the abolitionist movement against slavery and in the civil rights movement. And today churches still protest when the government ignores people who are poor and vulnerable.

Interesting. I'm curious, though, would Luther have agreed with these decisions to protest and disobey the government?

That's a difficult question to answer. As we've mentioned, Luther has a hard time imagining society running apart from some form of government. And it's important to keep in mind that in his day there are few models of what government can be like beyond the princes, emperors, and magistrates. At the same time, though, Luther supports a political alliance between a variety of German princes over and against the emperor to protect the ongoing Reformation.

Even though the emperor was the "authorized" leader? Doesn't that go against Luther's sense that government should be respected?

Yes, and both his respect for government and the need to at times resist government, if it acts in ways consistently contrary to God's will to care for all people, are found in the Bible. In his letter to the Romans, in particular, Paul stresses that government plays an important role ordained by God to keep the peace (Romans 13:1–7). At the same time, there is a story in Acts where the apostles defy the orders of local religious authorities to stop preaching and teaching. Interestingly, when they are questioned why, they reply, "We must obey God rather than any human authority" (Acts 5:29). Christians, including both Luther and Bonhoeffer, have taken that to mean not only religious authorities but also governing authorities.

That's interesting, but it also makes things complicated.

Definitely. One more thought: the key in questions dealing with how Bonhoeffer or, for that matter, how we might act in a given situation might not be to ask whether Luther would agree—after all, he lived five hundred years ago in a world very different from our own. Rather, we can ask how Luther's theology supports or informs the decisions we are making today. Bonhoeffer, a Lutheran, was trying to be faithful not to Luther but to his theology and, even more, to the gospel of Jesus Christ from which Luther's theology arose. If we continue talking about Luther, we'll see that he himself didn't always live up to his own theology, and to honor him for his insights into the gospel, we at times need to critique very strongly some of his decisions and actions.

Like in the Peasants' War?

Yes, and there are, unfortunately, other instances as well. If, that is, you still have more questions.

Oh, I definitely have more questions. Speaking of which, this has all been very helpful, and I appreciate the time we've taken to think it all through. But I remember that we launched down this path about God's two hands when I asked you how the first use of the law actually works in the world.

I remember.

You said the answer had two parts. The first part is that God is at work doing first-use-of-the-law kinds of things through institutions, and we've spent some time working that out and also how the "left-hand" institutions of government and family and all the rest relate to the "right-hand" institution of the church. So I'm wondering: did I miss the second part of the answer, or has all of our conversation been an exploration of just the first part?

We're still on the first part of the answer to your important question. And that's fine, because the question of how God works through institutions is both important and complex, and I've enjoyed thinking it through with you. At this point, I'd suggest that we take a break and then return to the second part of the answer, because that will also draw us more deeply into Luther's understanding of the Christian life.

Sounds like a good idea.

Insights and Questions

CHAPTER 5

Called for Good

*Vocation, Sinning Boldly, and the
Respiratory System of the Body of Christ*

Okay, we just spent a good deal of time talking about how God is at work in the world through institutions. This was the first part of what you said was a two-part answer to how God takes care of the world.

Right.

We looked in some detail at the institutions of family and government, remembering that "government" is best understood fairly broadly to include all kinds of public and civic institutions. These institutions help us take care of each other and restrain us when we only want to look out for ourselves, what we've called "first-use-of-the-law kinds of things." And we looked at the church as an institution where the second use of the law is at work and the gospel is proclaimed so that we hear and trust in God's promises to accept us, forgive us, and be with us.

Excellent summary.

Speaking of the church, though, I've got a quick question.

Hmm, most of your questions haven't been all that quick.

True enough. But here's my question: Is the church an institution? I mean, I get how it's similar to institutions because it's set up and run by people, like the other institutions we've talked about, but it's also kind of set up and run by God. So is it accurate to call it an institution?

Yes, the church is an institution. Keep in mind that Luther thinks *all* institutions are set up or at least authorized by God to do God's work in the world. Sometimes it's harder to see that in government agencies, other civic institutions, or families than it is when a pastor is offering forgiveness, preaching about grace, or baptizing a child. But we have institutions in both the "right-hand" arena for God's work in the world through the church and in the "left-hand" arena for God's work in the world through government and family. The difference is focus.

Focus?

Yeah. The church, in its primary role, has what we might describe as a spiritual or eternal focus on our relationship with God, while the government and family focus on what Luther would call temporal or material concerns, like our immediate physical needs and our lives with each other.

I need help with this. What's "temporal"?

It simply means "of this time" or even "in time," as opposed to those things that stretch into eternity, like our relationship with God.

So the church focuses primarily on our relationship with God, and the government and family focus on our relationships with each other.

Yes, and the key word is *primarily*. Our faith greatly informs how we view and treat each other, and we've examined how the church can support and correct the government, and how government can support or correct the church, always in the attempt to get each to do its primary work better.

In other words, not a "wall" of separation but a distinction between arenas of influence.

Right. Interestingly, Jefferson talks about "a wall of separation" between church and state in a letter he writes to the Danbury Baptist Association, in Connecticut, in 1802. He may have been drawing on the work of Roger Williams, the founder of the first Baptist congregation in America, who writes in 1644 about a "hedge or wall of separation between the garden of the church and the wilderness of the world."

Sounds like the superiority-thing of the church over the state at work again.

It could be, though it might also be Williams's way of saying that God's work is more orderly, or at least seen more clearly, in the right-hand work of the church than in the left-hand work of other institutions. Either way, I think the word *hedge* might serve us better. Hedges are definite boundaries, not easy to get over, but are more permeable than a wall, and they maintain a sense of interdependent independence.

Cool, that's helpful. Now maybe we can move to the second part of Luther's answer about how God is at work in the world.

Actually, I think we're already getting there.

How so?

Well, as you said just a minute ago, one of the main things that constitutes an institution is that people occupy it.

That seems obvious.

Perhaps, but also important. Institutions provide a certain amount of structure to get things done, but they're pretty much useless unless those structures are occupied by people. Churches, families, government, hospitals, relief agencies, food shelters—all are run by people. And that brings us to the second part of Luther's answer about how God works in the world. First, God ordains and authorizes institutions to help us take care of each other. Second, God calls individuals to get involved in these institutions to make them run and do their proper work.

I suppose I should get used to this, but I have to say that's not what I was expecting.

What were you expecting?

I'm not sure. Maybe it would help to hear more about what you mean by individuals being "called." I get that institutions are filled by people, but it feels like that's a natural part of institutions, and I'm not sure what special role God plays beyond simply authorizing them in the first place. Or maybe it's that I'm not sure what's important about the individual as opposed to the institution itself and what would warrant holding it up for special attention.

Fair enough. Okay, all those institutions we talked about—families, government, relief agencies, and the rest—are filled by individuals working together toward certain goals, which means that each individual has the ability to make a given institution better or worse. To refer back to one of your big questions from our earlier conversation, if you're part of a corrupt government, you can work to make it better. That seems to make individuals important. Institutions, as important as they are, don't run themselves. They run because of people, and people can make them run better or worse.

I get that. But if you're in a corrupt institution, it feels like it's a lot easier to talk about making it better than to actually do it.

No doubt! But still important to remember. Institutions, as we've been saying, provide the structures that make it possible for individuals to work together toward shared goals for the public good. That, in turn, means that the individuals in those institutions are really important. Every day, each and every person has the choice to make the particular institution they work in better or worse.

Again, I see what you mean, but sometimes it seems really difficult for one person in a corrupt—or even just dysfunctional—institution to make much difference.

I hear you. But it happens all the time. The whistleblower at a corrupt agency. The CEO who sacrifices immediate profit for long-term benefits. The worker who notices how something can be improved.

And this is why our individual choices and actions are so important.

Exactly, and it underscores again why church is important and how it can shape our lives in the world and, further, how God works through both the right and left hands to accomplish God's work in the world.

Really? How?

We've stressed the role of the church to work through the law and gospel to tell us that God knows us and loves us, and that is indeed its primary function. But the church also has a role to teach us the first use of the law, so that we know what God expects from us and, in particular, how we should care for each other. Moreover, church should be a place where Christians can come together to think through various challenges we face, and support and encourage one another to do the very best job we can in the various institutions we're a part of. I mean, if we confess that God is at work in the world through institutions, then we should probably expect church—the right-hand place where we probably talk about God the most and see God at work most easily—to give some shape to our lives in the left-hand institutions of family and government.

Interesting.

Luther believes each person is called at baptism to a life of caring for others and, for that matter, the whole world. And so an important part of church is to help us see how God works through us by equipping us to serve each other and the world through the various roles we play and stations we occupy.

Okay, here we need to slow down. First, what does baptism have to do with any of this? I thought baptism was mainly for babies.

This is indeed a great place to slow down. Baptism, according to Luther, is where God first makes a promise to us to accept us completely, love us unconditionally, and forgive us always. It is the mark of initiation to becoming a Christian, and has been throughout Christian history, and it is something most of us do for our kids when they're very young.

So far so good. This definitely sounds like a right-hand kind of thing. But what does it have to do with left-hand institutions?

While there's a lot more we could say about baptism, and maybe that will be helpful later, right now it might be enough to say that, like Luther's insight on justification by grace, baptism doesn't only free you from having to worry about whether God accepts you or whether you're worthy of love, baptism also frees you to live in the world.

So baptism is connected to justification?

For Luther, just about everything we're talking about is connected, and God's promise to justify us by grace is at the center of it all. So, yes, baptism is connected to justification. In one sense, baptism is the physical embodiment of justification by grace through faith. It speaks this promise, not only through words, but also through the physical element of water. Luther thinks the physical part is important, because it's a good reminder that the God who took on physical flesh in Jesus came to love, save, and bless physical people like you and me.

Got it. And that helps me appreciate baptism more. But I'm still not sure of the connection between baptism and God's ongoing work in the world.

Think of it this way. Baptism is God's way of speaking to us clearly, reliably, and tangibly—the physical thing again—of God's great love for us. It's not that God didn't love us before we were baptized, and it's not that God wasn't speaking to us through the words and deeds of those taking care of us since we were born, but it's that baptism is this kind of official, formal, or, maybe better, *authorized* word of God's declaration to us to be with us and for us forever. One of the primary reasons we baptize babies is so that the grace and love and acceptance at the heart of baptism are among the first words we hear, even if we're too young to understand them.

I'm with you so far.

Baptism not only promises that God will forgive you the rest of your life but also that God will go with you wherever you go and work through you in whatever you do. Baptism, in this sense, first promises that your relationship with God is secure—you never have to worry about whether God loves you. Then baptism sends you out with a sense of purpose that God will use you to care for your neighbor and the world, and the freedom to give it your best shot, because you've been promised that, no matter what happens, God will forgive you.

I think I'm beginning to see what you mean about the connection between baptism and justification, because this is beginning to sound a lot like the freedom *from*—death, fear, not measuring up, and all the rest—as well as freedom *for*—meaningful life in this world.

Exactly. In baptism, we hear the initial and physical promise of being freed *from* sin and death as well as being freed *for* lives of meaning and purpose. In this sense, baptism is the place where God first calls us.

God calls us. You've mentioned "call" and "calling" before, but say more.

Sure. God calls us in baptism in two senses of the word. First, God calls us God's beloved children so we'll know our identity as those God loves so much that God was willing to send Jesus. Second, God keeps calling us to use that gift and identity to carry God's love into the world.

I think I'm beginning to get it.

And the second part of Luther's answer to your question of how God is at work in the world is precisely through this second sense of calling. Each and every day, God calls us to be engaged with, committed to, interested in, and helpful to the people we meet and to the world we live in.

We're called to do a lot!

It is a lot, which is why this sense of God's calling has sometimes been called the second of the "twin pillars" of the Reformation. In a lot of ways, it's justification by grace lived out in our daily lives in the world.

I have to say I like this idea of "calling."

Luther does too, and it occupies a huge part of his theology. Since his time, we often refer to this dimension of his theology as "vocation," which stems from the Latin word *vocare*, which means "to call," and is also connected to the Latin root *voc-*, from which we get our word "voice." God calls us through baptism to lives of meaningful service to our neighbors and to all the world.

Interesting. I always thought vocation described your job if you're lucky enough to really like it, or maybe a hobby you enjoy.

We do use "vocation" in that sense. And it's not a bad place to start, because our callings are often connected to things we really enjoy.

But I think that misses the sense of being, well, called. Not just liking what you do but being called to do it, with a sense of purpose and urgency.

Yes, in the Christian tradition vocation is also connected to a sense of need; that is, God always calls us to help and support others, to respond to needs in the world. Frederick Buechner, a popular Christian author, has described vocation as "the place where your deep gladness and the world's deep hunger meet."[1]

Nice! I like that. But it raises a question. What if I don't like what I'm doing? Or what if I don't see how it connects to a deep need in the world? Do I still have a vocation?

That leads to a very important point. One of the mistakes Christians have often made is linking vocation to occupation. Actually, "mistake" isn't quite right. Our jobs often can be places of our calling. But Luther doesn't intend to limit vocation to occupation. Some of our most important vocations have nothing to do with paid work.

Really?

Sure. Think how important being a good parent is. Or, for that matter, being a good child, especially as your parents grow older and need your support. Or a good sibling, or a good friend. Life would be much more difficult if we weren't surrounded by people living out their vocations through their roles as family members and friends.

That makes sense, and, again, Luther's theology is a lot more relational than I would have imagined.

Definitely. And it doesn't stop there. You can find your vocation, your calling, through volunteer activities as well as through your other relationships.

That makes sense too. When I was in the sixth grade I struggled with math, to the point of nearly failing, and my teacher suggested I participate in an after-school tutorial program. It was staffed entirely by volunteers. One of them, a retired engineer, totally opened up math to me so that I not only passed the class but came to really like math.

Great example.

That helps answer my question, as I can see that even if I don't like my job, I can find other places to respond to God's call.

That's very true and important to remember. But it's also important to recognize that there's something dignified and holy about just doing a job well and bringing home an income. When we use the term "calling," we often think of helping professions like doctors, nurses, teachers, and so on. And, of course, these can be callings. But not everyone has a job they enjoy, and not everyone, as you said, sees how their job connects with needs in the world. But even in these jobs, there's a sense of calling in doing it well and, through your work, of being able to provide for yourself and those who depend on you.

My mom worked for years at a job she didn't like, to help put me and my brother and sister through college. I didn't know she didn't like it until after she retired, and mentioned it almost in passing. I knew it was a sacrifice, but I didn't think of it as a calling.

Absolutely. If there's one thing missing from the Buechner quotation, perhaps it's that sometimes it's not your deep gladness that meets the world's need, but your sacrifice.

I appreciate that. And I like how this sense of calling can lend a sense of purpose, and even dignity, to almost anything we do. I bet this was a pretty popular part of Luther's theology.

In some quarters, definitely, but not in all. In fact, to some folks it was pretty revolutionary and even threatening.

Really? Why?

The church of Luther's day had a strong sense that some things were callings, while other things were just work. And the callings, the things that "counted," were essentially religious types of work. The more religious you were, the more of a calling, or vocation, you had, which meant that while it was fine to be a mother or father, it was better to be a priest, and even better to be a monk or a nun. So when Luther comes along and says that our ordinary roles and tasks are just as important to God as the "religious" things we do, it doesn't go over all that well. To some of his contemporaries, Luther's sense of vocation seems to diminish the "holy" work of priests, monks, and nuns.

And what did Luther say about that?

He would have none of it. To make his point, he repeatedly emphasizes the incredibly ordinary things in life as places where we respond to God's calling—things like giving someone a haircut or changing diapers.

Changing diapers, really?

Oh, yeah. In one of his essays he writes that when a father changes his child's diapers, it makes God smile.

I didn't realize fathers did that kind of thing in the Middle Ages.

Typically, they didn't. In fact, what Luther really says is, "When a father goes ahead and washes diapers or performs some other mean task for his child, [even though] someone ridicules him as an effeminate fool . . . God, with all his angels and creatures, is smiling."[2]

Sounds like Luther chooses something as ordinary, even menial, as changing a diaper, then goes even further by choosing someone who wouldn't have normally done this work, to make his point that anything can be a vocation.

Right. Luther believes that God calls us by baptism and equips and encourages us through our life of faith in the church to serve each other and the world through pretty much any and all of the various roles we play and stations we occupy.

"Stations"—I remember you mentioning that once before. What do you mean by that?

"Station" in the sense of the place you hold in an institution, or the position or office you occupy. Being a parent is a station, as is being the treasurer for some volunteer group, as is being a police officer or an employee. The German word Luther used for this was *Stände*, which is the root of our word "stand." So I think of stations, positions, roles, or offices as the places where we take our stand in the world to do the will of God, help God's children flourish, and care for the world God loves so much.

The places where we take our stand. I like that. And this brings out the importance of the various things we do and roles we play.

Absolutely. As you said, it lends a certain dignity to the ordinary, everyday, and even mundane things we do. Luther would likely go a step further and say it actually lends a certain holiness to our everyday lives and work.

Interesting, and a little surprising. I mean, I tend to associate holiness with religious kinds of things, not everyday-life things.

To be *holy* essentially means to be set apart for God's work, which is why we often associate it with stuff related to religion. But once you recognize that God is super-invested in our everyday lives and gives us the law to take care of each other and to help us get the most out of life, then you realize that if you do any job you have or role you play in a way that helps others, it suddenly becomes holy.

That raises another question.

Fire away.

What about people who aren't Christian? Or people who don't even believe in God? Do they have a vocation?

Absolutely. Christians believe that God is the creator and sustainer of all things. And part of the way God continues to sustain the world

God loves so much is through institutions—not just the church but through institutions of the world, including institutions that aren't set up by or run by Christians. The same is true for the people who fill those institutions and do good work through them. In fact, Luther would rather have a non-Christian do an important job well than a Christian do it poorly.

So it doesn't really matter if you're a Christian? God still works through you?

God still works through you, even if you don't believe in God. But I wouldn't say it doesn't matter if you're a Christian, because our life of faith in the church can help us see our vocation and equip and encourage us to respond to it. Church, at its best, is a place where we are reminded of God's baptismal promises to love, accept, and forgive us; then we're sent out into the world to love and serve.

Freedom from and freedom for.

Exactly. But whether you recognize it or not, God is still using you to care for others and the world.

Sometimes I'll see a small cross on a billboard advertising a mechanic or doctor, and I always figured that was their way of telling people they are Christians and, I suppose, maybe saying that they are more trustworthy, or at least that they hope other Christians would come to them.

Sure. But whether you're looking for a mechanic or a doctor, Luther would urge you to find the best one you can, Christian or not. And, in turn, he would urge you, as a Christian, to be the best mechanic or doctor or parent or friend you can be. That, for him, is a big part of what it means to be a Christian—to hear and respond to God's call to care for your neighbor and the world.

I like that. But is there anything that can't be a vocation? I mean, are there any exceptions?

Anything done in faith and for the sake of another can be a calling. That rules out things that are illegal and things that take advantage of someone else for your benefit.

What if you do something that's illegal that helps others? Like Bonhoeffer and people who helped Jews in World War II Germany escape the Nazis?

When the laws of the land clearly contradict God's law to love and help other people, we're called to follow God's law, even if it means breaking the laws of the land.

That's helpful, and I see your point. Beyond those extreme situations, we're called to work within the institutions God has set up to help others.

And responding to God's call during a time of injustice and oppression not only achieves some immediate good, like helping someone escape the Nazis, it also provides a witness to the injustice of human-made law in relation to God's law.

A witness? Like in a trial?

Sort of. At a trial, we want witnesses to tell the truth.

The truth, the whole truth, and nothing but the truth.

That's right, and sometimes breaking the law serves as that kind of truth telling. That's what Martin Luther King Jr. did through his civil rights protests. He broke laws, and by suffering the consequences—being put in jail—he drew attention to the injustice of all those laws about where African Americans could sit or eat or get a drink, and other unjust laws too.

That makes sense. But it raises another question for me. King didn't take the law into his own hands, but by suffering under an unjust law showed—or, as you said, provided a witness to—how unjust those laws were. He lived out that vocation peacefully. But some vocations aren't peaceful. At least not all the time. Earlier we talked about police and fire departments being an example of institutions that help us live together, and a minute or two ago you mentioned the role of a police officer. Even though police officers are there to keep the peace, sometimes they use force to do it. And that often doesn't seem all that Christian. I mean, the first part—keeping the peace—does, but the second doesn't.

I see what you mean. And Luther does too. In fact, he writes an essay to discuss this aspect of vocation called "Whether Soldiers, Too, Can Be Saved."[3]

Yes, that's it exactly. So what does he say about this?

For Luther, what makes all the difference is whether you are holding an office.

An "office"?

By "office" I mean an authorized position within an institution. A police officer holds an office. So does a soldier. And so do doctors, for that matter, and school teachers. Those offices all authorize the person holding them to do certain things when they are in that position. Not anyone can pull someone over for speeding, only a police officer can, by virtue of his or her office. Similarly, not anyone can write prescriptions.

But people in those offices do those things because they're qualified, right? I mean, they've been trained.

Training often is a requirement for holding an office. But it's the office itself—the office you may have to be trained for—that holds the authority. Take, for example, the U.S. president. Once presidents are out of office, it doesn't matter if they don't like particular laws Congress is proposing; they can't veto them. And they can't sign bills, or do a number of other things they previously did while in office.

Because those things belong to the office, not to the president as a person, no matter what experience or training a former president may have. And that's true for soldiers and police officers too.

Yes. Offices are set up to help us seek the civic welfare through the institution authorizing the office.

Like the government authorizing the president to sign bills into law.

Right. So in the case of the soldier, Luther says that when he thinks of killing someone, it doesn't seem remotely Christian and indeed breaks God's commandment against murder. But for a soldier, functioning out of an office set up to protect people, especially the vulnerable who cannot protect themselves, even something as awful as killing may be the right thing to do to protect others, because that is part of the office the soldier occupies.

So it's not only Bonhoeffer, for instance, who is fulfilling a vocation by opposing his government and breaking unjust laws to save people from the Nazis, but also the soldiers of the Allied forces who fought a deadly war to stop the Nazis from spreading their hatred across the world.

Yes. But it's important to be clear that sometimes figuring out how to respond to God's call through baptism isn't straightforward or unambiguous.

What do you mean?

Just that when we talk about vocation, it can sound too easy sometimes. You just do your job—as a parent, doctor, police officer, soldier, and all the rest—and God works through you. Clean and simple. And often it's like that, but sometimes it's not. Sometimes it's really hard.

Can you give an example?

Plenty. As a parent, how do you balance how much time to spend with your kids and how much time to spend at work providing for your kids? Or, when your child is struggling with homework or some challenge, when do you decide to jump in and help out, and when do you give them advice and support them in their struggle, and when do you stay out of it altogether and let them figure it out so they don't become dependent on you? Those can be really hard decisions, and there are no clear "right" or "wrong" answers.

I see what you mean.

Doctors have to make similar decisions. When do you recommend surgery? How do you choose a course of treatment when none stands out as clearly the best? Or as a police officer, when do you stop someone? When do you issue a warning rather than a ticket? In the most difficult and dangerous of circumstances, when do you pull a trigger? Police officers sometimes have to make really, really difficult decisions, often under pressure, and with life-and-death consequences.

No question, and to be honest, I hadn't thought of that. But each and every week we have to make decisions that, while not always life and death, are still complicated, and we often don't have clear answers. And sometimes the consequences are huge. So what does Luther have to say about that?

At least two things. First, we're not called to be perfect and, indeed, we can't be. We're called instead to be faithful. And part of being faithful is being ready to make what I'd call a "reverent best guess."

Interesting phrase. Explain it some more.

Sure. By "reverent," I mean that we're called to talk it over with other Christians and consider whatever decision we're facing from the point of view of our faith, and of course we're invited to pray about it as well. By "best," I mean getting as much information as we can so we are better prepared to make an informed decision. But even once we've done all that, we still have to admit that sometimes we just don't know the best course of action. We make a guess, not totally in the dark, but a guess nevertheless.

Reverent best guess. I like that. But what about when we're wrong? Like we've said, sometimes being wrong isn't such a big deal, but sometimes it has life-and-death consequences.

That leads me to the second thing. Even when we've done our best, but make mistakes or fail, there may be consequences. Being a Christian doesn't remove those. We're expected to take responsibility for our actions. But that doesn't change the fact that we were acting in faith. You can be, in other words, both faithful and wrong. So while there may be actual consequences for you and others from your decisions, your relationship with God is still intact. You're still free to respond to God's call and decide how best to do that, hopefully being encouraged when you get it right, and learning from your mistakes when you get it wrong.

That makes sense, but it still isn't easy.

Definitely not. A good friend of mine, a doctor, told me about a time when he had to choose between two very different options for a surgery that was not going as intended. He had very little time, consulted with the doctors around him, prayed, and made a decision. It didn't work, and the patient died. He said he carries the memory of that loss every day, but he also carries with him the knowledge that he gave it all he could and has been forgiven.

Forgiven? It seems strange to talk about forgiveness in this case.

He came up short and felt terrible about it. Forgiveness isn't simply about doing something wrong. I mean, given the situation and that there was no guarantee the other option would have turned out differently, you could argue that being wrong or taking the blame wasn't really the issue. Forgiveness, though, is more about relationships than it is blame, and it helped him to know that his relationship with God was intact. In fact, that God not only forgave him but also would continue to use him. In this sense, forgiveness freed him to move on, learn what he could, and try again, even though he knows he might face similarly complex situations in the future.

I understand more about being faithful but wrong, and the difference between consequences and our relationship with God that frees us to try again. But I have to say that it feels like a whole lot of pressure.

Sometimes it is. But that's what makes God's promise to forgive and accept us *no matter what* all the more important. Again, we're called to be faithful, not perfect. Which reminds me, actually, of the story behind probably the most famous—and definitely the most misquoted—thing Luther ever said.

Which is . . . ?

"Sin boldly."

I've heard of that. I assume it means if you're going to sin, you might as well go big. Like, instead of stealing a piece of candy, steal the whole box.

I think most people think of it that way. But that's not even close to what Luther meant.

127

I'm ready to be enlightened . . . and, I suppose, surprised yet again.

Okay, so let me set the context first.

Sounds good.

Luther has recently been excommunicated for his refusal to recant his writing.

Okay, you said something about this before. Luther is asked to recant—to take back what he had written.

Right. Luther is offered the chance to say that his books were in error and he shouldn't have written them.

But he doesn't, so he's excommunicated, essentially thrown out of the church.

Yes. He can no longer receive communion and is banned from the services of the church. In the medieval world, where every time you sin you're back in a mortal state of peril, not being able to confess your sins, receive absolution, and take communion meant you were pretty much going to hell. When Luther receives the official letter from Rome with the pope's seal and everything, telling him he's excommunicated . . .

. . . Luther throws a party, builds a bonfire, and burns the pope's letter.

Good memory! Yes, and now there's a price on his head. So Frederick the Wise, the powerful German prince who's protecting him, has Luther kidnapped while on his way back home from a debate in another city.

Kidnapped?

Think of it as a friendly kidnapping, more or less to throw folks off the track.

Clever.

Yup. And then he has Luther hide out in the castle of another town and wear a disguise and everything.

Sounds like a TV drama!

It was, though he isn't sprung in the very next episode but instead stays hidden for more than a year.

That must have gotten boring.

Probably, though he makes good use of his time. He writes three of the most famous essays of the Reformation and translates the New Testament from Greek into German.

Sheesh, the guy is nonstop.

You could say that. In any event, during this time, the Reformation he started in Wittenberg is struggling.

How so?

As is often the case in any kind of movement with strong personalities, factions begin to develop as people want to see the Reformation move in different directions. Luther has the kind of *uber*-strong personality that could keep most other folks in check, but in his absence, things quickly begin to fall apart.

So who's running things while Luther is gone?

Several reformers keep things going. One of the most interesting is Luther's friend Philip Melanchthon. It's actually a lost letter from Philip that occasions Luther's remark. Philip, you see, feels a huge weight of responsibility to do his part to help keep things running well. But things aren't going well, and what's worse, Philip feels pulled between two factions. One group wants to speed up all the reforms they can think of, because they believe the Reformation isn't going nearly fast enough, and the other wants to slow everything way down because they're worried they're losing too many people because of the pace of change.

That sounds like a lot of groups I've been a part of! Which one is right?

That's the problem: there is no clear right or wrong choice. So Melanchthon writes Luther this anguished letter laying out all his fears, essentially saying he feels like any choice he makes will be wrong, cause the Reformation to fail, and it will all be his fault.

Yikes, sounds like he's stuck. And, for that matter, pretty hard on himself and, if it's not wrong to say so, maybe just a little too timid.

Well, it's a bit hard to say. History hasn't always been kind to Philip. He's sometimes considered the lightweight of the Reformation, or at least folks thought he was the least courageous and most cautious of the reformers. But I think that, to be fair, we should keep in mind that Melanchthon is only twenty-four at this time.

That's really young.

Yeah, and this is his very first reformation!

Ha! I hadn't thought of that, but you're absolutely right. Okay, Melanchthon gets a pass. But I'm curious, what does Luther say in response?

Well, first he says that he thinks Melanchthon is too preoccupied worrying about committing fictitious sins.

Fictitious sins?

Sins that are fictitious because they aren't about what's actually happening but about what might happen or could happen or even probably will happen.

But couldn't we just call that being cautious? As we said, decisions have consequences. So what's the problem?

The problem is that Philip's stuck, overwhelmed by these concerns, and can't do anything. Moreover, Luther said, the other problem is that God doesn't forgive fictitious sins, only real ones. And the thing is, there's no way Philip is going to get through this thing without making mistakes. He will sin, and God will forgive, but right now he's paralyzed by his fear, so he can't do anything good for anyone.

And that's why Luther says, "Sin boldly."

Right. Sin bravely, in confidence that God will forgive you. But Luther also said something else that usually gets forgotten: "Sin boldly, but believe and rejoice in Christ even more boldly."[4]

Rejoice and believe more boldly. I like that. It's like we're back to the "freedom from" and "freedom for" again but with more muscle.

What do you mean?

Well, we're not just called to live but to live with courage, to throw ourselves into the world—our jobs, families, relationships, projects, everything. And we don't need to get stuck worrying about the future, because God has given us lots of things we can draw on to do this, and God has promised to forgive us even when we make mistakes. It's kind of Luther's take on Nike.

Help me out on that one.

Like we said, it's important to study and pray and prepare and all that, but in the end, you're called finally to "just do it."

Ah, I see—yes, that's it exactly. To move forward, even to compromise.

Compromise. I didn't see that coming.

Absolutely. Each and every day we're faced with all these decisions, and even when we see what we think would be ideal, we can rarely achieve it. So we're regularly faced with a choice—compromise or do nothing.

I have to say I've never thought about compromising being a virtue.

But it definitely can be. In government, in business, in making decisions about your time with family, in choosing how much to donate to the causes you support.

Sin boldly.

Right. So we pray, study, and make our best guess, and then count on God's forgiveness.

Or, in other words: sin boldly, but rejoice and believe even more boldly.

Exactly. And then we do one more thing.

Which is?

We get our tails back to worship the next week so we can hear those words of forgiveness and be reminded that God loves us and wants to make use of our gifts and roles, then sends us back out into the world to love and serve our neighbors.

Which brings us full circle, back to church again as the place you can count on to hear God's love and acceptance, and God's call to us sending us back out into the world. I like it.

That back and forth—from church to the world and back to church again—gets repeated each and every week for millions of people, all potential agents of God's love and good purposes.

Agents of God's love and good purposes. I like that too. And I appreciate that it's not static. Too often it feels like church is a place where not much happens. But the way you're describing it, with this in and out, back and forth, church is constantly in motion, receiving and then sending, forgiving and calling. Constant motion.

Sometimes I think of this pattern as the respiratory system of the body of Christ.

Hmm. I'm not totally sure I'm following.

In the twelfth chapter of 1 Corinthians, Paul describes all the people of the church as members of the body of Christ. They—we—have all kinds of gifts and skills and experiences. We are made up of all different temperaments and backgrounds. We've got a variety of roles and opportunities. But we're all part of the same purpose, the same body, the body of Christ trying to extend God's love as far and wide and deep into the world as we can.

That makes sense, and it's a beautiful image.

Paul had a way with images.

And the respiratory system thing?

Well, bodies breathe in and breathe out to stay alive. And I sometimes feel like each week we're being breathed into church to be accepted, forgiven, equipped, and sent, and at the end of the service we're being breathed out again to love, care for, struggle, compromise, and more, all so that we can care for the world God loves so much.

The respiratory system of the body of Christ. I like that too.

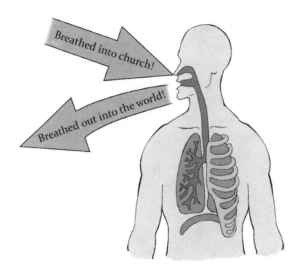

So does Luther. In fact, his twin convictions are that justification frees us *from* fearing sin, accusation, and death, and justification frees us *for* meaningful, purposeful life in the world.

Breathing in, breathing out; church and world; forgiveness and action. Like I said, I really like it. This is not what I thought church and theology were all about. Which, if you don't mind, brings me to one more question that's been nagging at me for a while.

Great. Let's take a break, maybe even breathe in and out a few times, and then come back to it.

Sounds good.

Insights and Questions

CHAPTER 6

God Hidden and Revealed

*Luther's Theology of the
Cross and the Sacraments*

So, you said you had another question that's been nagging at you.

Yes, and to tell you the truth it seems a little odd, even to me, but here it is: the more we get into Luther's theology, the more I find myself saying something like, "That surprises me," or, "I didn't see that coming." I guess that's the question: why is Luther's theology so surprising and unexpected?

That's a great question. We talked about this a little bit earlier when we distinguished Luther's theology from what we might call "natural theology."

I remember. Natural theology is the picture of God you'd come up with if you only looked at nature. So, for instance, because nature seems to be governed by the rule that "the strongest survive," we naturally assume God is all about power. And because nature can be chaotic, even violent when it comes to natural disasters or illness and all the rest, we assume that if God is more powerful than these things, then God must also be violent.

Good memory. And we contrasted that with Luther's theology.

Which starts not from what we'd expect—from looking at nature—but from what we actually see in Jesus.

Right. While Luther has great regard for the human imagination and for reason—that which gives us the ability to invent philosophies and compose music, for instance—he doesn't trust our ability to picture God. He sees in the Genesis story of human sin a profound and consistent confusion about God that continues to haunt us. So rather than look to nature, he looks to revelation as captured in the Bible and, in particular, to God's revelation in Jesus.

That makes sense. But didn't other theologians look to Jesus? I mean, surely Luther isn't the only one to read the Bible.

True. The church's whole history stems from its ongoing engagement with scripture.

Then what sets Luther apart?

Two things. First, I don't want to suggest at any point that Luther is the only faithful theologian. He, in fact, would be horrified by that idea. Doing something new definitely is not his intention. Rather, he wants to get back to what he believes were earlier and more faithful teachings of the church.

Which is why we call him a reformer, not a revolutionary.

Exactly. He pays great attention to the apostle Paul, for instance, and St. Augustine of Hippo, both of whom he finds very helpful. And afterward, other reformers like Melanchthon, John Calvin, and many others, while differing from him at points, also contribute much to our understanding of the gospel.

Okay, but I still find myself being surprised by his theology and wonder why.

That brings me to my second point. As we said, Luther learns through his own experience and eventually through his reading of scripture not to trust his natural instincts when it comes to understanding God. He begins, in a sense, to narrow down where he's willing to look. So rather than look to all of nature, he looks to scripture. And rather than look to scripture in general, he sees God's clearest revelation in Jesus, so he looks there. And while he pays attention to all that Jesus says and does, he gives particular and primary attention to Jesus' cross. Which brings us to another *sola.*

Another *sola*? As in *sola scriptura*, scripture alone, *sola fide*, faith alone, and *sola gratia*, grace alone?

Exactly. This one is *sola Christi*—Christ alone. For Luther, you see, Jesus' cross and resurrection not only serve as the climax to the whole of the biblical story but also provide a lens through which to read all of scripture.

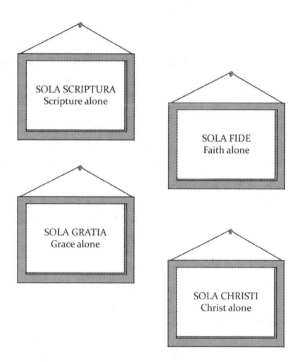

Hmm, slow down a bit. Climax? Lens? Can you say more?

Sure. Nearly all Christians believe that while God is not done working in the world, the climax and culmination of that work were and are through the life, ministry, death, and resurrection of Jesus. But Luther goes a little further, focusing particularly on Jesus' death on the cross, and seeing that event not only as the climax of God's work but also the thing that reveals the primary nature of God's character and disposition toward humanity. In this sense, Luther views all the other work of God—that described in the Bible as well as those things we might point to in history or our own lives—through the lens of the cross. In short, he tries to make sense of *everything* God does in light of the principal or *most important* thing God does in the cross. This is what I mean by saying the cross is not only a climax but also a lens.

I think I'm beginning to follow.

Maybe an example or two from the Bible would help.

Sure.

In the letter to the Hebrews, the author says, "Long ago God spoke to our ancestors in many and various ways by the prophets, but in these last days he has spoken to us by a Son . . ." (1:1–2). So what do you notice?

I guess what caught my attention was the contrast between "long ago" and "in these last days."

And what do you make of it?

The author seems to be saying that God is doing something different, maybe something new.

Yes. And it's not that the author is saying what God did before is wrong, or that the new thing is better. Just that it's clearer. The other contrast is between "many and various" and "a Son." The first is plural, God revealing God's self and work and purpose in a lot of ways: covenants, laws, prophets, judges, kings, and so on. While later . . .

God's Son is singular. I see what you mean about this being clearer. It's been narrowed down. This is the primary, singular way in which God is telling us what we need to know.

Right. And for Luther it all boils down to the cross.

Why? I mean, I know the cross is important, but why, specifically, is it so important for Luther?

A couple of reasons. First, it's clear that all the gospel stories point to the cross as, essentially, what they're building up to. After covering a couple of years or more in Jesus' life, the story in each of the gospels slows way down and gives us a day-by-day, almost hour-by-hour account of Jesus' journey to the cross.

Interesting.

Moreover, Jesus himself predicts his cross and resurrection three times in most of the gospels, and there are many parts of the story that foreshadow Jesus' death.

Like?

In the first chapters of Matthew's gospel, when the king and religious authorities plot his death. An angel warns Joseph, and Jesus gets away this time, but later in the story it's the same crew, political and religious leaders, who combine forces and go after him again. In Luke's gospel, there's this scene about Jesus' naming day when he's just a baby—again right near the beginning—when this old man named Simeon starts offering a prophecy about all the great things Jesus is going to do when he grows up. And right near the end of this, he looks over to Mary and says, "And a sword will pierce your own soul too" (2:35), looking ahead to the grief she will experience.

Really interesting, and it helps me see what you mean. Luther is saying that the whole Bible is helpful, but the part about Jesus is most helpful. And while all of the life of Jesus is important, what's most important is the part about the cross. That's where God is speaking most clearly to us.

Exactly. The speaking part matters. In fact, the reformers sometimes describe God as the *Deus loquens*, Latin for "the speaking God," the one who wants to be in relationship with us and so speaks to us.

So *loquens* means speaking?

Right. It's the root of our word "eloquent."

So Jesus—especially in his cross and resurrection—is where God speaks to us most eloquently?

Yes, that's it. Because in the cross, God shows just how much God loves us. Just how far God will go to save us.

Cool. Which makes it easier to understand why Luther feels the cross is so important—the climax and lens, as you said.

He thinks it's important for one other reason as well.

Yes?

Because it's about the last place you'd expect to find God.

What do you mean?

Well, like we said, we tend to expect God to be like everything else we see around us. So, if nature is powerful, unpredictable, and violent, we sort of assume—maybe not saying it out loud, but nevertheless kind of assume—that God is powerful, unpredictable, and violent. And that tendency to imagine God in the ways we experience nature makes Luther nervous.

Why?

On the one hand, it's understandable that we'd look to nature, to the creation, to understand God the creator. But Luther thinks we tend to look at creation to understand God in order to control God.

To control God? What do you mean?

We're limited in the ways we can control nature, but we can learn to adapt to it. We learn to read signs of the weather and take shelter when it's going to rain, seek shade when it's too hot, and so on. Or we figure out how to make fire and use that to improve our lives, and we invent things, whether the wheel thousands of years ago or, more recently, how to use atomic energy. In this sense we master nature by learning to adapt to and harness it to our ends.

What does all this have to do with God?

Well, Luther thinks our natural inclination is to do the same with God.

Control God? Interesting. Say more.

Sure. Maybe another story from the Bible would help.

Great.

Okay, so there's this pretty cool story where Moses is on the run . . .

Is this before or after the flight from Egypt and the ten commandments scenes we talked about earlier?

Way earlier. In fact, this is where everything gets started—the story of the burning bush.

I think I remember that one. Moses is out herding sheep and sees a bush that is burning but never gets burnt up, and when he goes closer to see it, God calls out to him.

That's right. And it's at just this point that God tells Moses to go to Egypt to rescue the Israelites. And instead of saying, "Cool" or "Awesome" or even "Okay," Moses says, "Tell me your name."

Really, why?

Actually, the first thing he says is, "Who am I that I should go to Pharaoh, and bring the Israelites out of Egypt?" (Exodus 3:11).

Sounds like he's either being humble or he just doesn't want to go.

I'm betting on the latter. And for good reason, as the pharaoh's incredibly powerful and probably doesn't feel like setting slaves free.

And what does God say?

God says, "I will be with you; and this shall be the sign for you that it is I who sent you: when you have brought the people out of Egypt, you shall worship God on this mountain" (Exodus 3:12).

And then Moses asks for God's name?

Yup. To quote the Bible exactly, Moses says, "If I come to the Israelites and say to them, 'The God of your ancestors has sent me to you,' and they ask me, 'What is his name?' what shall I say to them?" (Exodus 3:13).

Why does he do that?

There are a number of different interpretations, but I think there are two main reasons. The first is simply that there are a lot of gods in the Old Testament world, and Moses may want to make sure the Israelites get that he's representing theirs. But the bigger reason could be that Moses wants to get a handle on this God, perhaps even control God to some degree.

Control God? Just by knowing God's name? I'm definitely not following you.

I get it. There's a huge cultural difference between the world of the Bible and our own. Customs, traditions, and beliefs are often really different. And one of those differences revolves around names.

Names?

Yeah. In our world, a name is just a name. Maybe it has a connection to someone in your family, or maybe your parents really liked it, but your name is just your name.

And it was different in Moses' time?

In the culture of Moses' day, names revealed something of the character of the person. Which is why there's often this emphasis on names, especially when names change. So the "founder" or forefather of all the Israelites is originally called Abram, which means "exalted father." When God promises to lead Abram to a new land and create a nation from him—this is when Abram and his wife Sarai are really old and have no children—his name changes to Abraham, which means "father of many."

Interesting.

In this case, the name describes the promise of God to Abraham and the role he will play. At other times, a name reveals one's essential character. Jacob, for instance, literally means "heel," because he's holding onto the heel of his twin brother when he comes out of the womb. But it also means "following on the heels of" in a kind of negative sense. That is, it describes someone who's always trying to get ahead—in fact, to do whatever it takes. In this sense, Jacob means "the supplanter" or "usurper," and that pretty much captures Jacob's character.

Interesting. But I'm still not sure what this has to do with Moses and God.

Because names reveal your essential character, those who know your name have a certain hold on you. I mean, you can't get away with stuff because, well, they know you, know what to expect, and know how to deal with you. It wasn't uncommon at this time to have two names: one you used in work and everyday dealings with folks, and another that you shared only with your family and closest friends because it revealed who you really were.

Okay, this is beginning to make sense. So when Moses asks for God's name, it's not quite as innocent a question as it sounds. That is, Moses wants God to reveal God's character and give Moses a hold on God.

Exactly.

Clever. And what does God do?

This is where it gets fun. In response to Moses' request for God's name, God says, "I AM WHO I AM" (Exodus 3:14).

That's all? What kind of name is that?

Exactly. What kind of name indeed. It's totally not what Moses expects or wants. But it is kind of cool. It's essentially God saying to Moses, "Look, I'm God. I just am. I am pure being, pure life, no name captures me, so don't try to pin me down."

Yeah, that is pretty cool, and I guess captures things—about as well as you can capture them when you're talking about God.

It gets even better, because, actually, the Hebrew verb has a bit of a future sense to it and so we could translate it, "I WILL BE WHAT I WILL BE."

Which means God is totally free.

Right. Again, Moses can't pin God down and shouldn't try. But it also means that if Moses wants to learn who God really is, he's going to have to come along for the ride and see what God does. And at the far end of the exodus, Moses sings a song about God and uses the "I AM" name but then starts describing God by all the things God has done: the one who rescues Israel, the one who throws into the sea the horses and soldiers trying to recapture the Israelites, the one who saves Israel, and so on (Exodus 15:1–19). Moses discovers who God is by watching what God does.

Which is a lot like what Luther tries to do.

Exactly. And when God shows up in a way Moses never expects and refuses to be pinned down and thereby asserts God's freedom, Moses realizes that he can't control God, and at the same time he learns that he can trust God as the one who looks out for you and saves you.

And that's why Luther's theology is surprising? Even, well, predictably unpredictable?

Right. It's not so much that he's trying to surprise anyone with his theology, but more that he's trying with his theology to accurately describe the God he sees in Jesus. And what Luther sees in Jesus is the ultimate example of God showing up where you least expect God to be.

Say more.

Well, Jesus starts out by coming among us as one of us, being born as a baby. And if you know anything about babies you know that while they're cute, cuddly, lovable, and all that, they're also incredibly vulnerable.

Sure, they depend on their parents for everything.

Which is not what you'd expect from the God of the universe.

I'd never thought about that, but of course you're right. About the last place you'd expect the supreme being to show up is as a totally helpless, dependent, vulnerable baby.

The same thing keeps happening throughout Jesus' life. He doesn't hang out with the rich and famous, but the poor and outcast. He doesn't spend his time with the righteous, but rather the unrighteous and sinners, the folks "decent" people tend to avoid. And not only does that surprise the righteous and religious people of his day, it makes them really mad.

Why?

Well, I think what they want from their religious leader—maybe what we too often want—is to be affirmed, to be told we're doing it all right. But Jesus comes along and seeks out people who are lost and helpless and outcast. And it shows us that we've got a lot to learn, that God is more interested in finding and helping the people who can't help themselves than those who can, that maybe God isn't as interested in the things we value—like wealth or power or prestige—but is more interested in things like compassion and love and justice.

Interesting.

Then Jesus not only hangs out with outcasts and sinners, he forgives their sins. And that makes people really mad.

Why?

Because it messes with our sense of justice. We tend to think "bad" people should be punished and "good" people should be rewarded. So what happens when God just decides to forgive people?

Everything gets messed up. Who's in, who's out, who's good, who's bad. Forgiveness messes with all of that. It's like we build all these really cool, helpful—if also somewhat judgmental—castles in the sand, and the tide of God's love comes in and washes them all away.

You're right. It's not that our sense of justice and law and order and all the rest is wrong. It's just not enough. It doesn't leave any possibility beyond punishing each other endlessly.

Gandhi's "An eye for an eye makes the whole world blind."

Yes. But forgiveness, as we said, breaks the chain of cause and effect and creates the possibility for something new.

Love.

Right. And that's why Luther thinks God shows up where we least expect God to be. Because as much as we like to talk about love and to feel loved, we don't necessarily trust love because we're not sure it's as powerful as, well, power. Out of our human insecurity, we want law, order, and power, and God wants us instead to embrace, or at least receive, love and forgiveness. So God needs to surprise us, even make us give up everything we think we know about God and ourselves.

Which is why Luther's theology is surprising—because *God* is surprising. Moses couldn't pin down God, and neither can we.

If there's one thing Luther is sure of, it's that you can't control this God. And when you realize this, you finally have to give up and let God be God—the one who loves and saves. And you can just be you—not in control of God but a beloved child of God.

I like that.

While we talked about how God surprises us by coming as a baby instead of a warrior king, by hanging out with the "undesirables" instead of the famous and powerful, and by forgiving people instead of punishing them, the number-one thing we'd least expect God to do is to die as a forsaken criminal on a cross set up on a junk heap outside Jerusalem. But that's exactly what God does.

And no one expects it.

Not then, not now. The apostle Paul called the cross "foolishness" (1 Corinthians 1:18), as in absolutely ridiculous, you'd be a fool to believe it. But through this foolishness, Paul continues, God shows us that everything we thought was wise isn't enough, everything we thought was strong isn't enough, everything we thought was powerful finally isn't enough to save us and the world.

And once we've realized that, maybe we'll give God's offer of love and forgiveness a try.

It's painful when the things you counted on don't work, but it's effective, as you finally abandon hope that you can save yourself and let God save you.

This reminds me of the first step in Alcoholics Anonymous and other twelve-step programs: you realize you are not in control. And until you realize that,

you won't let God or anyone else really help you, because you don't even want to admit you need help.

I think that's pretty much it.

So, now I think I see why the cross is so important to Luther. It's absolutely the last thing you'd expect God to do and the last place you'd expect God to be. When you realize that's what God is doing and that's where God shows up, you just have to give up and surrender to God's grace and mercy, instead of always trying to do it yourself.

In some ways, Luther's whole theology can be called a "theology of the cross," and he himself wants to be, as he calls it, "a theologian of the cross," because he believes that the cross finally tells the truth.

. . . the truth about us and the truth about God. Like we said when we were talking about law and gospel, the law—in its second use—shows us the truth that we can't save ourselves, and the gospel shows us the truth that God can save us and, in fact, wants to and will.

That's it.

I like how Luther's theology is all kind of interconnected and hangs together.

That's right. Essentially, justification by grace through faith, law and gospel, and a theology of the cross are all different ways of describing what it's like to meet the God of love and forgiveness in Jesus.

And God's love and forgiveness hold it all together and help you make sense of your life.

Yes. If you follow this pattern of God's surprising grace even further, you begin to make sense of everything else Luther is trying to say.

Like how God's two kingdoms, or really God's two hands, are kind of like law and gospel assigned to our relationships with each other.

Exactly. Or how the sacraments, baptism and the Lord's supper, are kind of like Luther's theology of the cross coming to physical expression.

Whoa, I hadn't really expected that. I suppose I should be used to saying that! But, honestly, I think of baptism and communion as, well, religious

practices or rituals, which might be meaningful and important and all that, but I don't think of them as surprising.

That might be because we don't always teach them all that well. But they are.

Okay, you've got my interest. Keep going.

Sure. We've talked about how there were seven sacraments that were recognized or sanctioned in the church of Luther's time.

And Luther narrows them down to two. I remember, though I'm not sure why.

Luther wants the sacraments to be both reliable and tangible sources of God's grace and freedom. Later Lutherans follow his lead and emphasize that typically a sacrament should have three attributes: it's commanded by Jesus, accompanied by a physical sign, and conveys the promise of grace and forgiveness. And when you use those three criteria, baptism and communion are the two that stand out.

Interesting. Why those three criteria, in particular?

First, I should say that Luther isn't terribly strict in applying those criteria. He and other reformers often call confession and absolution the "third sacrament." With regard to the first of the three criteria, commanded by Jesus, Luther tends to be pretty suspicious that the church—and humanity more generally—isn't satisfied simply sharing or even mediating God's grace but rather wants to be in charge of it. So he feels that we often make sacraments of things that, while good—like marriage or confirmation, for instance—aren't necessarily commanded by God. Luther thinks that by making all these other things sacraments, the church has sort of taken the sacraments out of God's hands and into its own. He wants to get back to those things that Jesus commanded.

Fair enough. And the physical sign?

Two reasons. First, the two sacraments that Jesus commands each have a physical sign or element attached. In baptism it's water, and in the Lord's supper, or communion, it's the bread and the wine.

Makes sense.

Second, Luther feels this is no accident. This is part of the way God tends to convey grace to us most fully.

I'm not sure I follow.

Think of it this way: In the incarnation, when God comes to be among us in Jesus' human flesh, Luther sees God's commitment to truly and completely be one of us, so that we can trust that God is also with us and for us. And if that's true of Jesus, Luther thinks it's true of the sacraments too. That's part of what makes them so important. They are signs of God's love, forgiveness, and grace that we can touch and feel, that we can even eat and drink. They're physical, like we are.

That's pretty cool. Like God is making provision for us. It's not all just words and ideas but something tangible, physical, like we are. I like that.

Definitely.

So commanded by Jesus—check. Physical sign—check. And the third is . . . ?

Conveys the promise of God's grace and forgiveness.

Right. I should have remembered that. We've already said Luther's theology all hangs together. And it seems like grace is pretty much at the center of everything Luther does.

Absolutely. Grace changes everything. It does for Luther, and it does for us. And so, the third thing that makes something a sacrament is that it clearly and reliably conveys God's promise of grace and forgiveness. In fact, for Luther, it's this promise connected to the physical element that makes a sacrament.

Say more.

Sometimes people will bring water back from the Holy Land and want to use that for a baptism, or they'll insist that only the very best wine should be used for communion.

Really? Judging from the wine we use, I don't think anyone at my church has insisted on that!

Maybe not. But what I mean is that sometimes people think what matters most is what you use in the sacrament—holy water or special wine or whatever. But what really matters is that God has added the promise of grace and forgiveness to the sign.

Got it. In fact, baptizing with ordinary tap water could be a good reminder that God comes in the sacraments to promise love and forgiveness to ordinary people.

Exactly.

So, another question: baptism and communion are both commanded by Jesus, use physical signs, and convey God's promise of grace and forgiveness. Are they more or less the same thing? Kind of just repeating each other? Not that there's anything wrong with repetition, but how do they relate to each other?

Great question. And useful to know too. The sacraments are definitely similar in that they share these three attributes. But they're also distinct, and each is surprising in its own way. Baptism, for instance, is what we might call the "first words" or "original sign" of the Christian life.

"First words"?

Right. Partly because baptism is an initiating rite, the way a person comes into the church. And partly because these initial words, combined with the sign of water, are God's way of drawing us into the Christian family. Baptism is the start of the Christian life.

So is baptism what makes you a child of God?

That's another really good question. Luther would say baptism is not so much what *makes* you a child of God as it is what *tells* you that you are a child of God. That is, God loves the whole world and Jesus died for all people. But it's one thing for that to be true, and another to know that it's true *for you*. So baptism makes you a part of the Christian family, those who know of God's love in Christ.

Two friends of mine are expecting their first child. One didn't grow up going to church and so isn't really all that interested in having their child baptized.

But the other did grow up going to church and really, really wants the child baptized, like the baby's going to go to hell otherwise.

I know what you mean, and in some Christian traditions that's fairly common. As far as Luther is concerned, baptism is important, but not as a ticket to heaven. In fact, Luther recognizes that not everyone has the opportunity to be baptized and can't imagine that God holds it against people if they can't be baptized.

That makes sense and it's a relief. But why is baptism important then?

It's important—really important—because in baptism God says to each of us, personally, that God loves us and promises to be with us and for us forever. God promises salvation to us in baptism. That doesn't mean God won't save those who aren't baptized. Think about it this way: we are all born children of God the creator, but in baptism we are *told* that we are God's own beloved children and that God loves us enough to send Jesus to show us God's love, even to the point of dying on the cross.

I see what you mean. Telling someone something matters because it makes it more believable and more real for them.

Right. I mean, imagine growing up and never having your parents tell you they loved you.

That would be rough. And maybe they did love you—they provided for you and cared for you and helped you through some tough times and everything. But there's something powerful and important about being told that you're loved.

I agree. And baptism is also important because it's where we receive a new name.

A new name? I'm not sure I've heard about that.

Actually, the name you receive is the name of Jesus, of Christ.

This still isn't ringing any bells. Can you explain?

Sure. A while back we talked about how Jesus is the one person who lives in perfect relationship with God and in perfect harmony with God's will. He is sinless, perfect, holy.

Right. Which is why the church in Luther's day thought he had racked up so many extra credits, or merits, that we can dip into those through our good works.

Good memory. Well, Luther takes that a little further, saying that what happens at baptism is not simply that you're forgiven once and then have access to Jesus' merits going forward. Rather, he believes that at baptism God promises to regard you as if you were Jesus— just as perfect, just as holy, just as sinless and blameless. And that promise lasts as long as you live.

Seriously? God treats us just like Jesus?

Yes. The apostle Paul, who has a great influence on Luther, says something similar in his letter to the Romans. Paul says that because baptism is God's word and promise, it affects us, works on us, and makes a difference in our lives. And he says we are children of God, and not just children but heirs.

Heirs?

Yes. We haven't earned or worked for or achieved it through our own effort, but we receive an inheritance simply because we are God's children.

That sounds like grace!

Exactly like grace. Here's how Paul puts it:

> For all who are led by the Spirit of God are children of God. For you did not receive a spirit of slavery to fall back into fear, but you have received a spirit of adoption. When we cry, "Abba! Father!" it is that very Spirit bearing witness with our spirit that we are children of God, and if children, then heirs, heirs of God and joint heirs with Christ—if, in fact, we suffer with him so that we may also be glorified with him. (Romans 8:14–17)

So, if I heard that correctly, Paul goes a little further. We're not just heirs in general but *joint* heirs with Christ!

Exactly. Luther believes that in baptism God promises to treat us as if we were just as good, perfect, blameless, and holy as Jesus is. Heirs.

Like heirs to the throne! As if each one of us is some kind of prince or princess, but we just don't know it yet.

Well said.

But here's the thing: does baptism *make* us into Jesus—perfect—or at least better? Because, to be honest, I'm not like Jesus. Maybe I try. And on some days I think I do pretty well. But I'm not perfect.

I know what you mean.

Don't get me wrong. I'm not some ax murderer either, but I'm not Jesus. So, I hate to put it this way, but is baptism just a bunch of words?

That's an interesting way of framing the question. Is baptism just words? Does it actually *do* anything? Well, first off, think about how powerful words are. And, in particular, think about how powerful names are. Names like "stupid," "ugly," "dumb," "loser."

I get it. In fact, my mind just went back to middle school when we first got really, really good at slinging names at each other. And you're right. Those names are really powerful. It feels like our parents lied to us at some point.

What do you mean?

Most of us at one time or another had a well-intentioned mom or dad say to us, "Sticks and stones can break your bones, but names can never hurt you." Then you get to sixth grade and realize names are way worse than sticks and stones.

Definitely. And this is why baptism matters. Because names don't just hurt, they also heal, and they can make you stronger and, over time, change you. Names like "beloved," or "darling," or "child." These names are also powerful.

I see what you mean.

Now consider that it's God saying this. God, the creator and sustainer of the universe who also knows that you exist, cares about your ups and downs, and makes a promise to you when you are baptized that God will always be with you, always care for you, always love you, and always regard you as holy, blameless, and pure—just like Jesus—no matter what.

Wow! When you put it that way, I can see why Luther thinks baptism is so important. It actually affects us, makes a difference.

I think it also helps to remember it's "not just words" because Jesus didn't just talk about love, he died on the cross to demonstrate just how much God loves us.

Can you say more about that?

Sure. Some people think of the cross as a kind of mechanism, a way by which Jesus made it possible for an all-just God to forgive us by giving God someone to punish instead of us, namely, Jesus. But others think that it's because God is *already* loving and forgiving that Jesus takes on our lot and our lives in the incarnation, shares God's word of forgiveness even when it makes people mad, and eventually dies on the cross, all to show us just how far God will go to convey God's incredible love. In this sense, the cross is more of a physical, visible, and powerful message about God's love.

Message rather than mechanism. I like that.

And I think all this helps us to get at your question about whether baptism makes us more like Jesus. Again, Luther trusts the power of words, and especially the power of God's word spoken so clearly and forcefully in the life, death, and resurrection of Jesus. And so he believes while God's promise is, in a sense, delivered to us all at once anytime we hear it, over time that promise tends to make us more like what we have been called.

Interesting.

Here I want to be clear: God calls us and treats us like Jesus from the beginning, so we are completely and fully justified right from the beginning. There's no waiting for that. At the same time, we may experience the depth and power of being God's beloved children more fully over time.

Call someone awful, and they probably become more awful. But call someone beloved, and they become more lovable.

Right, although not like magic, but because it's through words and names and the relationships they establish that we create and nurture our identity.

Got it.

When I was in grad school, for instance, one of my professors would regularly refer to me as "Doctor." Which was nice, but it also made me a little uncomfortable because I hadn't earned the degree yet, and on some days wondered if I ever would. Eventually I asked him why he did this. He said that in the African American church in which he grew up, you called a person not just what they were but what you believed they would become.

Powerful!

Exactly. That naming helped empower me to finish. Someone believed in me, and that belief shaped my identity. His words weren't just nice, they were powerful; they shaped who I was becoming.

I think I see what you mean.

And the name and identity God gives us in baptism are that of Christ.

Again, I really like this, being called "Christ."

That's actually one of the names for baptism.

What do you mean?

Luther tends to prefer the word "baptism," largely because that's what it's called in the Bible. And that word comes from a Greek word that means "to cover."

So in baptism we are covered by God's grace and love.

Exactly, covered over by the waters of baptism, which convey God's enduring grace and love. Some Christian traditions have another name for baptism, though. They call it a "christening."

Yeah, I've heard that. In fact, that's what the friends I was talking about call it.

Christening has come more generally to mean any kind of naming—like when you christen a ship—which is another reason Luther and his followers preferred *baptism*. But originally christening meant just what it sounds like. That is, to be baptized is literally to be *Christ-ened*—to be given the name of Christ.

Cool. I definitely did not know that.

So baptism is important to Luther because at the very outset of life, or whenever we might be baptized, we hear God's promise made publicly and personally to us that God is with us and for us and regards us as God's own beloved child, just as beloved and perfect and holy as Christ is.

That's a pretty incredible promise.

Which is why Luther thinks it's so important to remember. Every worship service that begins with the words "In the name of the Father and the Son and the Holy Spirit" is essentially reminding you of your baptism, because that's the name into which we baptize.

I had no idea.

And every service that begins with confession and absolution is a reminder of the forgiveness and grace of baptism.

I didn't know that either.

Luther believes you can't be reminded of baptism too often. Which is, again, why the physical element of water matters. Every time you wash or go swimming—or use water in any way, for that matter!—you can be reminded of just how much God loves you.

Awesome.

All of which is why I referred to baptism earlier as the "first words" of the Christian life, not simply a rite or ceremony that brings you into the church, like you're joining some kind of club, but rather because Luther wants those to be the first and primary words you hear.

Is that why Lutherans baptize babies? I have another friend who's pretty adamant that you shouldn't baptize anyone until they're old enough to understand it.

Yes, some Christians sometimes refer to the "age of consent" and talk about "believer's baptism" as opposed to "infant baptism."

That sounds familiar.

The emphasis for these folks is on our ability to accept God's love, to invite Jesus into our hearts, and to take responsibility for deciding to become a Christian. They want to underscore that becoming a Christian should be our own decision and choice, not just something our parents do for us.

Yeah, that's the way I've heard it explained. And I have to say it makes some sense. I mean, we want people to understand what's going on, right? I have to say that I don't even remember my baptism.

I see what you mean. But let me ask it this way: do you remember the first time your parents told you they loved you?

No, of course not.

Would you have preferred that they waited until you understood just what love means? Or until you understood and could appreciate how much they love you?

Again, no. And I think I see what you're getting at.

For Luther, as important as it is that we grow into an understanding, or at least an appreciation, of God's love for us, it's even more important that we grow up just being able to count on it, hearing it over and over, even if we don't yet understand it. Like a parent's love.

That makes sense—a lot of sense, actually.

And I think infant baptism is also important because it reminds us of who's really in charge of all this.

What do you mean?

In the end what matters most is not that we understand it, or that we accept it, or that we choose it, or that we "invite Jesus into our hearts," but rather that God does it for us. There's something really powerful, I think, about God coming to us before we can understand, let alone make a decision, and just plain declaring that we are God's own beloved child and God is our loving God once and forever.

Kind of audacious, when you think about it.

Can you say more?

Well, God doesn't wait for us to make up our minds but just barges in and says, "I love you, like it or not." Which is really cool, when you think about it. God takes responsibility for this relationship, so it's the only relationship we can't blow.

I think you're right. On a day-to-day basis, it matters whether we appreciate God's relationship with us or not, but because it's ultimately God who establishes this relationship, God is the one who will keep it intact even when we neglect it.

Okay, I think I've got it. And, like you said earlier, it really is like what we called Luther's theology of the cross—God showing up just where we least expect God to be. I mean, all these powerful things of naming and identity and belonging and all the rest hidden in the ordinary water and promises of baptism. Not what I'd expect, but cool.

I think so too.

And what about communion? You said this is surprising as well.

Only if you think it's surprising that you receive the real presence of Jesus each time you take communion.

Okay, I see what you mean by surprising, but I'm not sure I'm following you. Let's slow down a little. What do you mean by "real presence"? Do you mean we're really eating Christ's body and drinking Christ's blood? To be honest, that sounds a little gross. I always thought we were just kind of being reminded of those things.

Interesting you should put it that way. In the medieval church, pretty much the dominant—if not only—way to think of communion, which is also called the Lord's supper, is that in this meal we are receiving Christ's actual body and blood, and the things we're receiving only look like bread and wine. And later in the Reformation, others conclude, like you, that that's not too appetizing, or at least goes further than you need to go, and so they describe communion as remembering Christ's sacrifice. And for most of the church's history ever since those have been the two main options.

And which side does Luther come down on?

Neither.

Neither? I suppose I should have expected that! So what *does* Luther think is going on in the Lord's supper?

Great question, and to answer it I'm going to start with the Greek philosopher Aristotle.

Okay, I'm game.

So Luther grew up with the Roman Catholic view that in the Lord's supper the priest changes the bread and wine into Christ's body and blood. This is usually called *transubstantiation*. It gets its name from Aristotle's distinction between the substance of a thing and its accidents.

Substance and accidents?

The substance of a thing is its essential being. What it really is at the core. And the accidents are the particular attributes it has when you experience it. Take a chair for instance.

A chair?

Yup. When I say that word, you probably know exactly what I mean.

Sure. Something you sit in.

Yet you've experienced hundreds of different chairs over your life. Wood chairs, metal chairs, plastic chairs. Soft chairs, hard chairs, plush chairs, flimsy chairs. All those different attributes are the accidents, the particular characteristics of an actual chair. But beneath all those different accidents of all those particular chairs there's still

159

a certain essence, or substance, of what a chair is that you immediately understand.

A chair's "chairness"!

Pretty much.

And that's what Aristotle means by substance and accidents.

Right. And that's true not only for chairs but pretty much everything.

I think I understand. I've got a golden retriever, and she's furry, kind of cinnamon colored, medium sized, friendly, and all. That's different from my sister's German shepherd, which is very different from my neighbor's Yorkshire terrier. But even though the accidents of all those particular dogs are different, they all share a certain "dogness."

You've got it.

But how does that apply to communion?

Well, the Roman Catholic view of all this is exactly what the word *transubstantiation* describes. During communion, the priest changes—"trans-" means change—the substance. It may still have the *accidents* of bread and wine, but its *substance* has actually been changed into Jesus' body and blood.

Okay, I'm with you so far—though it seems a bit of a stretch.

The other position, often called *memorial feast* because it focuses on remembering Jesus' words at the last supper and his sacrifice on the cross, more or less agrees with you. Instead of getting into all this stuff about bread just looking like bread and really being Jesus' body, it says, let's just call it what it is, bread. And let's assume when Jesus said, "This is my body," he meant it symbolically, and our job is really to remember his cross, because he also said, "Do this in remembrance of me."

Which is kind of where I would probably come down. But you said Luther doesn't.

Right. Luther is often seen as trying to find a compromise between these two positions. But he actually thinks these two options are not all that different, and he wants to call both of them into question.

Not all that different? They seem like polar opposites.

Maybe in the outcomes. But Luther thinks their assumptions are exactly the same.

Explain this a little more.

Essentially, Luther thinks the main question is whether something finite and ordinary, like everyday bread and wine, can hold or contain something infinite and eternal, like Christ's real body and blood. He poses this question with a Latin phrase, *finitum capax infiniti*: "does the finite have the capacity"—the Latin word *capax* is the root of our word "capacity"—"to hold the infinite?"

Interesting.

And, as far as Luther can tell, both of the traditions we're talking about answer "no" to this question. Those who advocate transubstantiation say, "No, finite bread can't hold the infinite body of Christ, and so it's not really bread anymore, it just looks like bread." And those who take the memorial-feast position agree, saying, "No, finite bread can't hold Christ's infinite body, so it's not Christ's body, it's just bread, a symbol to remind us of Jesus' sacrifice." But Luther answers the question differently: Yes, the finite can hold the infinite.

How?

Luther answers that in two ways. First, he says that the minute you deny the ability of the finite and ordinary to hold the infinite and eternal, you've more or less denied the incarnation. I mean, we confess what happens in Jesus' birth whenever we say the Nicene Creed that Jesus is both "fully God" and "fully human"—the finite and ordinary hold the infinite and eternal. The early church asserts this over and against various traditions that say, "Jesus wasn't really a human but rather a kind of angel or divine being who only looked human," on the one side, and, "Jesus wasn't really divine but only a human whom God blessed and used," on the other.

Which is very much like what the two different understandings of the Lord's supper are essentially saying. So, Luther argues that communion is like the incarnation?

Yes. His view of the sacraments in general, and the Lord's supper in particular, is very incarnational, God coming among us yet again in a form we can receive.

Got it.

Luther then goes on to say that God, as creator of heaven and earth, is in some way a part of everything. And because Jesus is, in the church's language, the Son of God, that's also true of Jesus. The statement in the Apostles' Creed, "he is seated at the right hand of the Father," doesn't so much describe a place, but rather conveys a sense of Jesus' authority. So Jesus shares all things with God and is part of all things too.

I think I'm following, though this is a lot to take in. Are you saying that God really is everywhere, in the forest and lakes and animals and all of us?

That is what Luther would say, that God as the creator of all things is also present in all things. But there is a crucial distinction for Luther: just because God is present in all things doesn't mean God is present *for us*.

Hmm. I'm not sure I'm following. What's at stake in that distinction?

Well, from time to time I've heard folks—especially when they've missed worship a few weeks in a row—talk about how they experience God just as meaningfully in the beauty of a sunset as they do when they're at church. And on some level, I get that. Sunsets are beautiful and God created them. But here's the thing: all the colors that make the sunset so beautiful are also present in the lava flow from the earthquake that destroys a village and ruins people's lives. God as creator may be present in both, but it's hard to see. It's ambiguous. So, Luther talks about God always being present in creation, but sometimes God is "hidden," that is, it's hard to see God's loving presence, and sometimes God is "revealed," clearly present for us in love.

Which again sounds very much like Luther's theology of the cross.

Right. We discover God showing up and revealing God's incredible love for us in exactly the last place we'd expect. And something similar is happening in the sacraments. God may be present for us in all kinds of things and people and places, but we have the promise that God *will* be present *for us* in grace, love, and forgiveness in the sacraments.

It feels like the issue, as we talked about with the cross, is clarity.

Right again. At one point, for instance, Luther says God is present in water, fire, and rope, but in a hidden way. After all, while all those things *can* be good, they aren't always. I mean, water drowns, fire burns, and rope hangs. In the bread and wine of communion, and in the water of baptism, God is not just present in general but present unambiguously *for us*. So Luther urges us to look for God where God has promised to be.[1]

Again, that's not what I expected, but it's really powerful.

Even more so when you think about what's at stake. By claiming that the Lord's supper can hold what Luther calls the "real presence" of Jesus, Luther reminds us that God keeps coming for us, not as the persons we're supposed to be, not as the persons we've promised to be, and not even as the persons we're trying really, really hard to be. Instead, God comes to us first in baptism and then again and again in the Lord's supper, just as we actually *are*—a mix of good and bad, dreams and failures, hopes and brokenness, but always and forever God's beloved people. We don't have to change to receive God, but as we receive God, we are changed more and more into the people God calls us to be.

That makes a lot of sense. Well, actually, in a lot of ways it doesn't make sense—that God would love us that much and keep coming to remind us in a way we can accept and grow to understand. But whether it makes sense or not, it's really awesome. God showing up where we don't expect God to be— first in the incarnation and cross, and then again in the sacraments—to surprise us, even to disrupt our sense that we're always in control, to remind us of God's love and root us in our identity as God's beloved people. Very cool.

I think so too.

Thanks very much for taking the time to explain this. It's all really helpful, and gives me a much deeper appreciation, not just for Luther's theology, but for how God is a part of my life every day.

I'm glad. I think that's exactly Luther's point—that we can experience God differently, in a new way, by understanding God in light of what happens in Jesus.

Having said that, I have just one more question. And this might be the hardest of all.

I've really enjoyed our conversation, and especially your questions, so I'll do my best to answer.

Insights and Questions

CHAPTER 7

Semper Simul

Sin, Forgiveness, and "Becoming Christian"

So, it sounds like you have another question.

Yes.

A hard question.

Yes again.

It almost sounds like you're not sure you want to ask it.

Well, I do, because I think it's important. But I don't, because I don't want to offend you.

I don't think that's likely.

You haven't heard the question yet.

We've been at this a while, and I've enjoyed your questions and getting to know you. Some of your questions, in fact, have helped me think more clearly about my understanding of Luther as well, and I'm grateful for that.

Really?

Absolutely. I find that conversations—at least real, honest-to-goodness conversations—are almost always like that. They push you, stretch you, draw you deeper into relationship with your conversation partner, and help you think more deeply and clearly as well. So, really, go ahead. I'll be grateful for the trust you're showing in asking what is clearly an important and difficult question.

Okay, thanks very much. So here's the thing: a few years ago I had a chance to tour the U.S. Holocaust Memorial Museum in Washington, D.C.

I've been there as well. It's a really well-done museum. Important, in many ways inspiring, but also really difficult—even painful—because of the subject matter.

That's the way I experienced it too. It's a huge museum—did you see most of the exhibit?

I went with my brother. We spent two full days there because we wanted to see as much as we could.

Then you probably saw the exhibits on the roots of anti-Semitism in Europe.

Yes. I have a hunch where you're going with this.

Well, here's the thing: I'm in that part of the museum, and there are various historical documents and artifacts from different periods of European history that help show the development of the anti-Semitism that eventually became front and center in Hitler's Nazi Germany and led to the Holocaust. There's one room set apart in this section where you can watch a film covering the topic. I went in to watch it, and right near the beginning I'm surprised and kind of upset to hear Luther lifted up as one of chief detractors of the Jewish people. I mean, he said and wrote some awful, appalling things! Not just prejudiced, but hateful, and not just hateful, but violent, recommending burning Jews' homes and driving them from the towns, all things that later happened when the Nazis came to power. I think I would have found Luther's words shocking no matter what my background. But because I'd grown up in a Lutheran church and always admired him—even if I didn't know all that much about his theology—I felt particularly appalled and offended, even kind of sick.

I had a similar experience. Even though I knew of Luther's anti-Jewish writings ahead of time, it really struck me how awful some of his language was. And when I compare his harsh words to the awful things actually done to Jews in Nazi Germany, it really makes me cringe. When I heard the words read out loud in that film, I not only felt sick, but also ashamed.

You said you knew of Luther's anti-Jewish writings before you visited the museum. Where do you find those?

Comments on the Jews can be found in several places in his writings, including personal letters. But three primary writings are most often quoted: *That Jesus Was Born a Jew, About the Jews and Their Lies,* and one with a really long title—*On the* Schem Hamphoras *and on the Lineage of Christ.* The first one was written relatively early in Luther's career (1523), but the other two were written twenty years later.

What kinds of things does Luther say in these writings?

In *About the Jews and Their Lies,* he suggests rulers set fire to synagogues and schools belonging to Jews, and tear down their houses. He also says the prayers and writings of Jewish teachers should be destroyed and rabbis forbidden to teach. And that's not all. He says Jewish people should not receive normal protections or be allowed to work as bankers. He even suggests the government should make young Jews earn their living through hard labor.

Wow, that is hard to believe. Are his ideas enacted?

No, fortunately at the time, most of these suggestions are ignored. Most of Luther's friends did not endorse his words or think they should be published. But that doesn't mean that anti-Jewish words and actions didn't happen.

So how do you cope with this? Or even, how can we take Luther—should we take Luther—as seriously as we have been when he also said these things?

That's a really good question. And I'm glad you asked it.

Really?

Absolutely. I don't think it helps anyone to celebrate the parts of Luther's legacy we find helpful and ignore those parts we don't.

I appreciate you saying that. I mean, I've found a lot of Luther's theology incredibly helpful, but this question has been nagging at me, and I'm glad we can get it out in the open.

Me too.

Here's the thing: We tend to like historical figures to be uncomplicated, either all good or all bad. But the more you read in history, the more you discover that people aren't like that. People are a mix of good and bad, pure and impure motives, altruistic and selfish moments, and all the rest.

You're right, and I think that's true of Luther too. In fact, there's a whole element of his theology that deals with this, and that part of his theology not only helps us to understand and even judge him but also to understand ourselves.

I'd be interested in hearing about that.

I'll tell you what. This is an important question, and to do it justice, I'd like to approach it from three angles—historical, temperamental, and then theological—if that sounds okay.

Sure. And not to jump ahead too much but, just out of curiosity, what do you mean by "temperamental"?

I'm thinking about who Luther was temperamentally, what his emotional makeup was like—at least what we know of that—and what was going on at the time of these writings.

Got it.

Okay. So historical considerations first. But two words of caution. First, there is no single view on Luther and his anti-Jewish writings, and there are heated debates both about the place of these writings in his career and his later influence on anti-Semitism in Germany and the rise of Nazism. I'll do my best to summarize the historical context and share where I stand on this, but others may feel differently and you may want to read more on your own.

Fair enough.

Second, we agreed before that it's not helpful to ignore elements of Luther's life and writing that we don't like. I think it's also important not to use historical and contextual explanations to excuse his writings.

What do you mean?

Just that I don't mean to excuse what Luther wrote and said by looking at the historical context in which he lived and trying to understand it. We'll do this carefully because we tend to judge someone like Luther by our contemporary standards, and there's something both fair and unfair about that.

I think I'm following you, but what do you mean by both fair and unfair? Maybe an example would help.

Sure. Take Thomas Jefferson, for instance. He wrote the Declaration of Independence, which includes this stirring line: "We hold these truths to be self-evident, that all men are created equal, that they are endowed by their Creator with certain unalienable Rights, that among these are Life, Liberty and the pursuit of Happiness."[1] And he wrote this . . .

. . . at the same time as he owned slaves. I see what you mean.

So, should we say, "Well, lots of people back then thought slavery was okay, so what's the big deal?"

No. Especially when lots of people around the same time *didn't* feel that way. Benjamin Franklin, for instance, was a staunch abolitionist, as was Alexander Hamilton and many others. In fact, even though Hamilton was an immigrant who spent most of his adult life in New York, a northern state, his close friend John Laurens was from South Carolina and also advocated freeing the slaves. So I don't think we can simply excuse Jefferson because of his context.

I agree. So should we say instead, "He should have known better. He was a racist slaveowner and therefore nothing else he did or said matters"?

Hmm. I'm not sure we should do that either. Jefferson did a lot of pretty amazing things, made a huge difference in U.S. and, for that matter, world history, and his words still ring powerfully true, even if he didn't live up to them.

I agree.

And while we're on this, even his best words could be improved.

What do you mean?

Just that he talks only about men. He doesn't even mention women. I know that was the convention of the time, but still, he could have done better. Especially when you consider that women didn't even get to vote until 1920, nearly a hundred and fifty years later.

Good point.

What's interesting about this is that there's something in Jefferson's writing—his declaration of inalienable rights, including the right to freedom—that allows us to critique his shortsightedness and failures with regard to both slaves and women. And I'm guessing you want to say something similar about Luther.

I do, though I think it will prove even more helpful after we put him in historical context.

Okay.

So, there's a lot of historical research on this area of Luther and not everyone agrees, but I think two things are important to lift up. The first is simply to recognize that many people in Luther's day were anti-Jewish, and that included many Christians. This prejudice had haunted the church for ages, and traces of it can even be found to some degree in some of the books in the New Testament.

Really?

Not like in Luther, but the seeds of those views can be detected.

I didn't know that.

In the beginning, almost all of Jesus' followers were Jewish. Eventually more and more non-Jews—or what they called "gentiles"—became Christians, especially through the ministry of the apostle Paul. But many early Christian communities were made up of lots of people who both followed Christ and identified themselves as Jewish.

What do you mean that there were Christians who also identified as Jewish? That seems contradictory.

Not at that time. Again, pretty much all of Jesus' original followers were Jewish, which meant they believed Jesus was the Jewish messiah, the one promised by the Jewish God, and so they thought they were fulfilling their Jewish faith. Over time, this set up a struggle between the Jews who followed Jesus and accepted him as the messiah and those who didn't. By the time the gospels were written—forty to sixty years after Jesus lived and taught—these tensions were growing more pronounced. You can feel some of this tension in the gospels written by Matthew and John, in particular.

Where, for instance?

Two examples. First, in John's gospel, a man who was born blind receives his sight from Jesus. There is a scene where the man's parents are very cautious while answering questions from the Jewish religious authorities. The narrator explains this by saying "they were afraid of the Jews; for the Jews had already agreed that anyone who confessed Jesus to be the Messiah would be put out of the synagogue" (John 9:22).

Wait, I thought you said they were all Jewish, so why does John talk about "the Jews"?

They pretty much *are* all Jewish. But John is distinguishing, as he says more directly in another place, between those Jews who follow Jesus and those who turn away or don't follow him (John 6:60–66). Keep in mind that while the gospels tell the story of Jesus, they aren't written as history books the way we think of them today. Rather, they are interpretations of Jesus' life written to encourage and strengthen the faith of believers who lived later. So the scene with the parents of the man who received his sight might be referencing something that was happening in John's Jewish–Christian community. Maybe people who had worshiped Jesus as the messiah in their synagogue were now being pushed out. This scene in John's gospel lets them know they're not alone and, even more, tells them they're the ones being faithful to their Jewish faith.

Interesting.

Think of it as a sibling rivalry. It's all one family, but the arguing can get kind of intense.

Yeah, I see what you mean. They're all Jewish but are arguing about who is the most Jewish or who is being Jewish in the right way.

Exactly. But much later, when there aren't two sets of Jewish traditions debating, but instead Christians and Jews, all this takes on a different significance, which leads me to a second example.

Okay.

When you read Matthew's description of Jesus' trial before Pontius Pilate, the Roman official who orders his death, Matthew goes pretty easy on Pilate, suggesting that Pilate wants to set Jesus free and is almost distraught that he can't. At the same time, in Matthew's gospel the Jewish religious authorities are the ones who really want Jesus condemned.

And that's not what happened?

To tell you the truth, we don't know what really happened. There's no question that Jesus ran into some serious difficulty with the religious authorities of the day, particularly when he criticized the temple. But it's not likely that the Romans would have gone easy on Jesus. They considered him an insurgent and revolutionary, and his critique of the temple also affected them—they collected a temple tax that was pretty important. We also know that Pilate was notoriously brutal and probably didn't agonize much, if at all, over Jesus' fate.

I see.

What's more important than figuring out exactly what happened, though, is paying attention to how all this gets portrayed in the gospels—and later in history. So, for instance, in Matthew's story, when Pilate says that he is innocent of Jesus' blood, the whole Jewish crowd calls out, "His blood be on us and on our children" (Matthew 27:25).

I'd never noticed that before, or at least how harsh it sounds now. This draws a contrast between, as you said, the Jews who follow Jesus and those who don't, by painting those who don't in a pretty unflattering light.

Right. Now, when Matthew wrote his account, the Christian community was really small, pretty insignificant, and perhaps was experiencing its own struggles and even being persecuted. In other words, it had next to no power. So if Matthew was feeling defensive about what we might call his sibling rivals, that might be understandable. But later, when Christians became the majority and held all the political power, these same words become justification for prejudice and discrimination. In fact, it's verses like these that led Christians to call Jews "Christ-killers."

That's awful!

Awful, horrific, tragic. You probably can't find enough adjectives to describe the pain these and similar scenes have caused. Matthew and John did not in any way intend this, and they could not have imagined how their words would sound centuries later or how they would be used, but what started as an intense sibling rivalry ended up preparing the soil for some pretty awful seeds to be planted and flourish.

And that includes Luther's prejudices.

Very much so. Which, again, doesn't mean he isn't to be held accountable for his views and words, but this puts them into context. And it also raises another historical issue.

Yes?

The question of whether Luther is anti-Semitic or anti-Jewish.

I'm not sure I understand the difference.

Anti-Semitism is a racial prejudice. Anti-Jewishness is a religious prejudice. Nazism was clearly a racial prejudice. Those who had any Jewish heritage whatsoever were persecuted, even if they had converted to Christianity. Most of Luther's focus, in contrast, is religious. Like some of the gospel writers, he feels Christianity is the "true" form of Judaism. He uses the Bible, including the Hebrew scriptures—the Old Testament—to argue that Jesus is the Messiah God sent to save all the world. Early in his career, Luther expresses hope that Jewish people will hear the gospel about Jesus and come to believe in him as the messiah. In his later writings, he becomes more mean spirited. He seems terribly frustrated and faults Jewish people particularly for what he considers their "failure" to accept Jesus as messiah and become Christians.

Okay, I see the difference. But I wonder, does it really matter? I mean, prejudice is prejudice.

Good point. You're absolutely right: prejudice is prejudice. At the same time, this question has mattered to historians, because it raises the question of whether the Nazis can be viewed as direct descendants of Luther. That is, were Luther and the later Nazis arguing for the same thing, or did the Nazis use Luther's anti-Jewish words to further their own anti-Semitic cause, including justifying the Holocaust?

And what do you think?

I think Luther's concern is largely religious, though at times he gets so worked up it's hard to tell the difference, and you can see why his words and writing became fodder for the Nazis. But earlier in his career he actually argues forcefully for better treatment of the Jewish people.

Really?

Yes, but to be honest it's not from what we might call humanitarian concerns but because he thinks the poor treatment of Jewish people has given them a bad impression of Christians and the Christian gospel. He says Christians have treated their Jewish neighbors so poorly that they've given them no reason to become Christian.

So both his earlier writings urging Christians to treat Jewish people better and his later writings attacking them are motivated by his religious goals.

Right. But at the same time . . .

Yes?

Well, I don't think there's any getting around this—and this moves us from historical issues to his temperament—the fact is, Luther's anger sometimes gets the best of him.

What do you mean?

He's passionate—well, more than passionate, fiery. And while this is part of why he's so effective, at times it proves to be an Achilles' heel.

Say more.

Luther is fiercely loyal to friends and allies, totally prepared to sacrifice himself for the cause of the gospel, and he could be incredibly generous and brave and kind hearted. But at times he uses very harsh, even hateful, language. We see this in his writings against the peasants, his criticism of Roman Catholic adversaries, his words against other reformers and Christians who opposed his direction, and his language about Muslims. Some of this was the rhetorical style of his day—people frequently attacked each other in harsh terms in their writing. But Luther really excels at this, and at times, it feels like he loses all sense of limits or boundaries.

Which is rarely, if ever, a good thing. I mean, I can see that it's in part his passion that makes him such an influential reformer, but it's easy to get into an ends-justifies-the-means mentality and forget that God loves even the people who disagree with you or who are different from you.

Exactly. And, in Luther's case, that passion—which is indeed a great source of strength for him—at times turns against him when the circumstances are more difficult.

What do you mean?

When you look at Luther's writing about the Jewish people, his views are pretty consistently biased against them throughout his career. But in his last years—his most hateful writing, called *About the Jews and Their Lies*, comes out three years before he dies—he is more and more physically sick and distressed, and he's more and more frustrated that the Reformation hasn't been successful. As a result, some argue that his outlook and writings become more hardened, even bitter.

Wait, what do you mean he's frustrated because the Reformation hasn't been successful? I mean, it pretty much changes European history!

But Luther doesn't know that. When he preaches his last sermon, just five days before he dies, only a handful of people show up, and he complains to some friends that he fears the Reformation has failed.

I had no idea.

And out of this sense of desperation, his writing, particularly with regard to the Jewish people, becomes more fierce, bitter, antagonistic, and violent. It's a tragedy across the board. More than a few folks who admire Luther wish he had not lived to write such awful things.

I agree with you that neither his temperament nor his circumstances excuse his writings. And I am grateful for the additional perspective, as it helps me make a little more sense of his writings and the dark legacy of how others used them.

It's difficult for us to recognize just how important Luther was to Germany. Earlier I compared his mixed legacy to that of Thomas Jefferson, but on second thought, I'm not sure that analogy quite does justice to Luther.

What do you mean?

Well, the writings of both Luther and Jefferson are hugely inspirational, but Luther is actually more important to Germany than Jefferson is to America. In many ways, Luther's more like George Washington, in terms of the near mythic status he holds. Luther establishes German culture and identity like it had never been before. For instance, before Luther, there had been all kinds of variations in the German language, but when he translates the Bible into German, that translation more or less standardizes the language. And when Luther stands up to the emperor, later Germans see that as a defining moment in their sense of national identity. Luther is a champion for public education. He composes hymns that most Germans grow up singing, he writes prayers everyone says, he publishes more than just about anyone in history, and in all these ways he becomes a symbol of national pride.

All of which, I imagine, gives everything he says—good and bad, beautiful and ugly—way, way more importance.

I think that's right. Which means that later, when the long-standing anti-Jewish sentiment of European Christians hardens into the racial hatred of anti-Semitism, his writings take on additional and terrible significance.

I appreciate taking the time to talk all this through. It was really difficult hearing Luther's words read at the Holocaust Memorial Museum, and it's been nagging at me ever since.

I think it's important to take the whole of Luther's legacy seriously. He's an incredibly important and, as we've seen, complicated historical figure. As with Jefferson, his worst moments don't necessarily negate everything else, but it's important to be honest about them.

I agree.

In fact, I'd go even further and say that only by being honest about Luther's failings, as well as his triumphs, can you really appreciate his theology.

What do you mean?

I mentioned earlier that in addition to looking at these darker elements of Luther's legacy from the vantage point of his historical circumstances and his temperament, I'd also like to think about them theologically.

I remember.

This seems like a good time to do that, because there are two elements of Luther's theology that sometimes get overlooked but are really important if we're going to take seriously what it means to be a Christian in the real world.

What do you mean by "real world"?

Well, sometimes religion can seem like a way to dodge, or at least sugarcoat, reality, but as we've seen at a couple of points, Luther is very much a realist. His definition of a good theologian—what he calls "a theologian of the cross"—is someone who "calls the thing what it actually is."[2] I think we've been trying do that with these difficult elements of Luther's legacy, and I think these two elements of his theology offer another perspective, not only on Luther but on our own lives as Christians.

Sounds good.

First, most of Luther's reformation is an attempt to shift the spotlight from what we are required to do to be righteous to what God has already done in Jesus to make us righteous. That is, Luther wants us to focus on what *God* is doing. But there are times when he gives up on God and when that happens things get ugly.

Can you say more about that?

Sure. From time to time, even though Luther has what often seems like incredibly strong faith, he gives in to despair. He writes about this, saying that the devil never stops attacking him. He has this struggle his entire life.

That makes me feel a little better about my own doubts.

Me too. And I think Luther ultimately gives up on God being able to keep God's promises with the children of Israel, and ends up thinking that he himself should be able to convert them.

You mean he thinks he has to take matters into his own hands?

Right. When the Jewish people don't follow his plans to convert to Christianity, Luther succumbs to the prejudice of his culture and faith and attacks them. At other points, he gives up on the Reformation being God's work, and thinks the whole thing is his responsibility. Then when he meets opposition or things aren't going well, he lashes out at opponents.

It definitely seems like there's a pattern.

All of which is an important reminder, I think, that we're not called to be successful but rather to be faithful.

Interesting. What do you mean by that?

I think Luther, at his best, wants people to follow Jesus, because in Jesus we see God's love and will for us and the world most clearly. And the thing is, Jesus doesn't always "win." In fact, he pretty much loses—at least according to how we usually think about winning and losing.

Maybe that's the point: Jesus wasn't out to win or lose but to show us God's love. I think that's the key—it's not about us but about God and how much God loves us. And bad things happen when we forget that.

Exactly. And there's no doubt that Luther knows this. He calls John 3:16—"for God so loved the world that he gave his only Son"—the "gospel in a nutshell" because his life changes when he becomes aware of the loving, parental God who justifies the sinner freely and gives us Christ's righteousness as a gift.

Right.

Luther also knows it's all up to God. When he's teaching on "your kingdom come" in the Lord's Prayer, he's really clear that God's kingdom comes on its own. We can't do anything to hurry it up or slow it down, and when you get right down to it, "your kingdom come" expresses our hope that God's kingdom comes to us and that we can be a part of it coming into the world.

But he forgets.

From time to time, pressed by difficult circumstances, shaped by medieval cultural prejudices, and perhaps haunted by his own demons, Luther totally forgets, or at least loses confidence in God's promises, and then takes matters into his own hands.

And by doing that he ends up in the same despair he experienced when he thought righteousness was up to him. Except he doesn't always turn that despair inward. Sometimes he turns it outward, and that's when things get ugly.

Exactly.

Which, truth be told, seems like something all of us do. Again, this isn't to let Luther off the hook—his influence was so great that his failures had enormous consequences. At the same time, though, I suspect each of us has moments when we forget to trust God, lose confidence in God's promises, try to take things into our own hands, turn too easily to despising those who don't see it our way, and just plain fail in our main calling to be faithful.

That brings me to the second element of Luther's theology worth remembering: the Christian life isn't about constant—let alone triumphant—progress.

I'm not sure I'm following you.

Many Christian theologians—and actually on this point I'd risk venturing that it's really *most* Christian theologians—tend to categorize the Christian life as an upward movement. That is, we're supposed to get better: "each and every day, better and better in every way." That is, we start as miserable sinners—or at least as sinners, depending on the tradition—then we meet Jesus, are converted, and begin a lifetime of moral and spiritual improvement. In fact, in this way of thinking, that's the point of becoming Christian: to get your life together.

I'll admit that that's more or less the way I assumed things work.

You're not alone. Like I said, this is the dominant picture of the Christian life.

And you're suggesting Luther doesn't think this is the way it works? That we shouldn't get better? I'll be honest; I'm a little confused. I mean, what's the alternative? That Christian faith makes no difference? Surely not that we get worse?

When we were talking about the sacraments, I said most people think Luther's view on communion is a compromise between transubstantiation and the memorial feast.

Yes, you said he wasn't trying to find middle ground but was actually advocating a whole other way of thinking about what's going on in communion—based on the incarnation and Jesus' promise to be really present for us in the bread and wine.

Right, and something very similar is going on here. Luther's not saying we should get better or that we shouldn't. In fact, he's not focusing at all on the effect of Christian faith on how we behave. Because he feels like if that's the focus you again shift your attention from what God is doing to what you're supposed to do.

That's really interesting. It reminds me of some friends of mine in college. They were part of a Christian fellowship group, and while they knew I went to church, I don't think they were convinced that I was "really" a Christian, so they'd invite me to their meetings. They were all very nice, but there was a lot of talk about "backsliding" and about making progress. They had a certain word for this but I can't remember quite what it was.

Sanctification?

Yes, that's it! How did you know?

It's a pretty important theological word in many Christian traditions.

What does it mean, exactly?

To sanctify something is to set it apart, to make it holy. And many Christians believe that the heart of the Christian life is to become increasingly holy, to keep getting better and better.

That kind of makes sense to me, but I gather Luther doesn't go for it.

You know, for Luther it really isn't a matter of going for it or not. It's more a matter of his absolute insistence on focusing first and foremost on what God does as the source of our confidence rather than on what we're supposed to do. And what God does is make us righteous.

Because righteousness is about being in right relationship, and only God can do that. So God justifies us by grace through faith.

Yes, you've got it.

But we still mess up. We still make mistakes. We still sin. Luther is a pretty glaring example of that.

That's exactly right. One way to look at things is that we sin, or have sin in us, or are dominated by sin—however you want to put it. From the point of view of sanctification, once we're converted—that is, come to faith in Jesus—we're now less sinful, or a little more holy, or on the road to being holy.

This sounds like the Christian life is like going to the gym. You decide you need to get in shape, you start working out, over time you get more and more fit. Maybe you have the occasional setback—a doughnut for breakfast instead of a kale shake—but by and large you keep getting in better and better shape. Except instead of fitness, we're talking about holiness. So is sanctification a kind of spiritual fitness?

That's really a pretty good analogy.

I'd say that all this makes good sense. So what does Luther object to?

I think it's not so much that he objects to it, but rather it's just not the way he thinks. Because, on the whole, this focus on holiness and sanctification doesn't end up being a very helpful or particularly accurate way to describe what goes on when God gets involved in your life.

Hmm. I'm not sure I see it yet. Say more.

I'd sum up things in two ways. First, this constant focus on getting more spiritually fit focuses nearly all your attention on yourself. What am *I* doing to get more holy? What do *I* need to do to get even holier? How am *I* doing in general? How am *I* doing compared to the people around me? Notice what goes missing in this litany?

God! I see what you mean. Your focus shifts—from what God has done and is doing—to yourself. But maybe people who think this way are concerned

about holiness precisely because God is holy and they want to be more like God, or at least more like Jesus.

Of course, but the moment-to-moment focus is on ourselves. Or, worse, because we never quite know how we're doing compared to God, we end up comparing ourselves with others.

And that rarely ends well. You either feel bad about yourself or judge the people around you negatively. It reminds me of our conversation about how self-justification leads to judging others.

Right. That's Luther's concern. This focus on becoming better and better, whatever its motivation, can easily lead to focusing on yourself—and self-justification and judging your neighbor—instead of focusing on what God has done and letting that free you to serve your neighbor. So it's not so much that Luther thinks this is all wrong, but just really unhelpful.

Got it. And you said it's not only unhelpful but also inaccurate?

Yup. Luther again provides a good—and terrible—example. As we've said, near the end of his life, instead of getting closer and closer to perfection, he ends up writing awful things about Jewish people. And it's really hard to say that these writings are just "backsliding."

And not at all like having a doughnut while you're watching your weight! I get it. It's not a minor mistake but an absolute failure.

And this failure is present for much of his life. His writing urging better treatment of his Jewish neighbors is more the exception to the rule, and motivated by the hope they would convert.

So how do we make sense of this? I mean, you're right, when you look at Luther's life it's not one glorious forward march of progress. There are huge lapses and, indeed, some evidence that in some things he was just wrong, and wrong all the way along. And, like I said before, if we're honest, our own lives are probably like that too. We're not on the steady road up and up with occasional detours. Instead, we can be really good one moment and really bad another, and some things plague us throughout our entire lives.

I agree.

So how is it that God gives us God's righteousness through justification, and yet at the same time we're still really caught up in, well, sin?

Luther uses a Latin phrase to describe this reality: *simul iustus et peccator.*

My Latin is really rusty!

No problem. It means that we are simultaneously (*simul*) justified (*iustus*) and (*et*) sinful (*peccator*, Latin for "sinner").

That seems to capture things pretty well. Particularly the *simul* part, but can you say more about where the rubber hits the road with all this?

Sure. The *simul*, as you mentioned, is key. It's not that we start out at 90% sinful and 10% holy, and a year or so later we're 60/40, and ten years later 30/70, and so on. It's that for our whole lives we are *at the same time* 100% sinful—insecure, confused, looking out for ourselves, not trusting God, and all the rest—and 100% righteous, because God keeps completely forgiving us, completely justifying us by faith, and completely giving us God's regard and righteousness.

Hmm, so God's grace doesn't really do anything? I mean, I know we talked about this earlier, but shouldn't it make more of a difference?

It makes all the difference in the world! It creates a whole new reality in which you can live. And, as we said earlier, when someone believes in you, forgives you, and loves you, it changes you. That change is more like creating a new reality for you to live in than erasing the old one.

This makes a lot of sense, even if it's not what I expected. But it's also a lot to take in. The 100% sinful and 100% righteous piece is still confusing. I mean, it seems to ring true, but 100 + 100 = 200. How can that be?

It is a lot to take in. I'd say God's grace draws us into a new reality, creates a whole new possibility for living with God and those around us, but it doesn't take us out of the reality we were born into. So both realities—old and new—are 100% present.

It's like what we talked about earlier, with King Lear living in England but asking if he was in France, because Cordelia's forgiveness didn't happen in his world.

Exactly.

Hmm. That makes me think of the way a friend of mine in recovery talks about his alcoholism. I mean, he is an alcoholic and sober and in recovery at the same time. And both realities—an *alcoholic* who is in *recovery*—matter. In fact, he's said that he's at his most vulnerable when he thinks he has his alcoholism beat and doesn't need to worry about it anymore.

That's another great analogy. And I suspect that's why AA meetings start with folks introducing themselves by sharing their names, then saying, "and I'm an alcoholic." It captures their two realities—their identity, name, and life in sobriety, and their alcoholism.

Yes, living two realities at the same time. And that's what Luther is getting at?

Right. Luther's trying to be as realistic as possible about the human condition and as realistic as possible about God's response to our condition.

The two truths—law and gospel again!

That's right. And the key to living with, if not escaping, the human condition is focusing on the gospel, on God's forgiveness and love for us.

It's really all fitting together. But I still wonder about how this *simul iustus* thing plays out in everyday life. I mean, it definitely describes things more accurately and helps keep our attention on God and all that. But one benefit of the sanctification approach is that it keeps your attention on doing what you ought to be doing. I mean, that's kind of what spiritual progress is about. And aren't we supposed to *do* things? Or at least do *something*?

> Definitely! But for Luther you don't need to be justified by grace through faith, or to be a Christian at all for that matter, to know what God wants you to do and do it. That's the work of the law . . .

. . . in its first use. I remember. The law tells us how to serve our neighbor so that all of us can live together in the world.

> Right. Once we're Christians there's no new law. And God doesn't want us to follow the law to earn brownie points or make God happy. Rather, God wants us to follow the law because the law helps us—all of us!—get the most out of life. When we realize that, and that God loves and forgives us, it creates in us the power to go at it again, to try once more to live as we've been called.

And when we screw up, to return to worship again, hear those words of grace and forgiveness, and be sent out into the world all over again.

> Right.

Which ought to pretty much guarantee good worship attendance!

> What do you mean?

Well, every week I screw up in one way or another. So every week I ought to look forward to coming back to church to hear that God loves me and sets me free to serve my neighbor and share God's love in the world, not because I have to in order to earn God's love or become more holy but because I'm free to. When I stop focusing on myself and recognize how much God loves me, it's actually easier to accept both myself and others.

> You're really getting it.

So, again, I appreciate taking the time to explore some of the dark sides of Luther's legacy. It's been difficult but also helpful.

You're very welcome. It's been helpful for me too.

What's particularly interesting to me is how these last two elements of Luther's thought sort of condemn Luther—or at least some of his really awful writings—and validate his theological insights as well.

What do you mean?

Just that at the heart of Luther's theology is God's action to justify us and our need simply to trust that. And, well, Luther fails. He despairs, loses confidence in God's promises, thinks he has to take matters into his own hands, and as a result says and writes terrible things. In this sense, he's condemned not so much by you or me but by his own theology.

I see what you mean.

But these episodes also validate his insight that we remain who we are—confused, insecure, sinful—even as God calls us and makes us righteous and holy.

I agree.

But in his worst moments Luther forgets all this. That we're not just *simul iustus et peccator* in general or from time to time, but always. Which means maybe we're actually *semper simul*.

Semper simul?

Yes. My brother was a Marine. Their saying is *Semper Fidelis*, "always faithful." So maybe we're *semper simul*, "always both" justified and sinful.

I like it!

And that's maybe what Luther forgets. And I suppose we all do at times. Which brings me to a final question: what do we do about that? How do we keep from making Luther's mistake? And, for that matter, what do we do about Luther's mistakes, his words and deeds that continued to haunt Germany and the world for hundreds of years?

I'd say that's not just one question!

Yeah, sorry about that. We can take them one at a time.

Well, the first is easy. Not easy in the sense that it solves everything, but easy in that it's the best strategy I know of to keep all this in mind. And that, once again, is to go to church.

I had a feeling you were going to say that!

Well, you said as much yourself. Our need to hear the gospel is a pretty strong attraction. And so is our need to hear both truths, about us and about God. I mean, the first thing you do in many worship services is confess your sin. And this isn't meant to be a "say how bad you are" moment but rather an *honest* moment, a realistic way to start the service. And the words of confession are simple, candid, and to the point: "We confess that we are captive to sin." And right after the confession, you hear that God forgives you.

Church, at its best, takes seriously both of our identities and helps us live out our new one, the identity of being God's beloved child sent out with a sense of purpose to love and care for those around us.

Absolutely. And it's not just the words said at worship. It's also being surrounded by other people who are also the *semper simul* children of God. Some you might know really well, others hardly at all, but there's something powerful about being gathered together, about confessing our confusion and sin together, about hearing words of grace and forgiveness together, about remembering our baptism and sharing communion together. It reminds us of our identity as the beloved people of God. Fallen, yes, but even more beloved.

I like that.

And it doesn't have to stop there. We can remind ourselves of our baptismal identity every time we wash or use water, as we said. We can read the Bible to be reminded of God's promises. We can sing hymns that set those promises to music. We can pray for the strength to remember them and to treat others as we want to be treated. All of this is good in person, but even better in company, and these are all things Luther advocates. In fact, he is one of the church's great hymn writers, precisely because he believes singing God's promises is one of the best ways to remember them.

That all sounds good. And the second question, what do we do about Luther's mistakes?

Repudiate them. That's first. And a number of Christian traditions—including the Lutheran tradition—have done so. Like recognizing that Jefferson and Washington were slave owners, this doesn't have to take away from Luther's accomplishments, but it's also important to recognize his failures, and be reminded not only that we're *semper simul*, as you put it, but also that God continues to work through even flawed human beings. You don't have to be perfect to go to worship, and you don't have to be perfect for God to do amazing things through you.

That makes sense.

But there's something else we *can* and really *should* do, in my opinion.

What's that?

We can also learn from and live into the best parts of Luther's legacy. And one of the best parts of his theology, as we've seen, is the belief that God never stops surprising us. God never ceases to do what we don't expect—forgive instead of scold, love instead of punish, offer grace instead of judgment. God just never stops showing up where we least expect God to be.

In a manger instead of a castle, and on a cross instead of in front of an army.

Exactly. And it doesn't stop there either. Jesus tells a parable or story about a king dividing all his followers into two categories: sheep who did what they were supposed to do by taking care of him when he was in need, and goats who didn't care for him. Most people read this as a morality tale: do what's right and go to heaven, and so forth.

Sounds pretty straightforward.

Interestingly enough, both the sheep and the goats ask, "Lord, when was it that we saw you hungry and gave you food, or thirsty and gave you something to drink? And when was it that we saw you a stranger and welcomed you, or naked and gave you clothing? And when was it that we saw you sick or in prison and visited you?" And the king responds to the sheep, "just as you did it to one of the least of these who are members of my family, you did it to me" (Matthew 25:37–40).

Okay, but that still sounds like it's about morality. You know, "Take care of people or else!"

Maybe. Or maybe it's a promise that God keeps showing up where we least expect God to be. In the manger and cross, in the bread and wine and water of the sacraments, as we talked about before. And in the face of our neighbor's need!

So it's like God is all around us, just waiting for us to recognize and honor God's presence in our neighbors by seeing that they're also God's children and offering us an opportunity to be in God's real presence!

Right. And when Jesus says, "the least of these," that certainly means those in great physical need. But I think it also means those who are the most vulnerable. Jesus, after all, spends most of his time hanging out with people who were considered socially undesirable. And while he sometimes calls people to follow him, sometimes he just sends them on their way. Sometimes, in fact, he doesn't even ask them to believe in him, like when he heals a Roman centurion's servant and praises him for his faith (Luke 7:1–10). Which makes me think that Luther had it backward when it came to his Jewish neighbors. Rather than try to convert them, he might instead have recognized God's presence already in them.

That's really interesting. And it seems like it has implications for today. I mean, we should definitely stand with Jewish people when they are being oppressed, but also Muslims, and maybe even those who don't believe anything.

Here's the thing: I think that when you read the Bible and Luther, you realize that pretty much every time you draw a line between who's in and who's out, Jesus ends up on the opposite side from you.

Because God is always showing up where we least expect God to be. But what about sharing our faith, evangelism? Aren't we supposed to do that?

Sharing, yes. Forcing, no. Evangelism is simply sharing what God has done in your life and why God's promises mean so much to you. The great commission in Matthew's gospel tells us to go and make disciples (28:19–20a). Disciples are people who follow. You can't *force* someone to follow, not really. Go and make disciples, baptize and teach. Our job is to share, to witness, and to love. It's up to God to change the heart.

It's God's responsibility, once again, like justification and righteousness and all the rest.

Right. And after the great commission comes what I like to call the great promise, when Jesus says, "I am with you always, to the end of the age" (Matthew 28:20b). That promise—that Jesus is with us and will take responsibility for changing people's hearts and saving the whole world—sets us free to care for our little corner of the world, starting with people we'd never imagine being the people God would choose.

Because God always shows up where we least expect God to be. Still!

Exactly. When asked about the Christian life, Luther said that the point isn't so much about *being* a Christian but *becoming* one, receiving God's forgiveness and justification anew every day. And this becoming doesn't mean a forward march of progress but allowing God's word and promise to sink into us more deeply. And as it does, we feel more and more free to take risks, even to make mistakes, but especially to love those around us. To see them as God's children and as opportunities to experience God, so that we can receive *all* the people around us—our family members and friends, and also neighbors and strangers—as God's gifts to us.

I like that.

And that freedom is, as we've said before, the heart of Luther's theology and Reformation.

By focusing on what God has done in Jesus and continues to do in us and the world, we are free from worrying about our relationship with God and also free for reaching out to care for our neighbors.

Right. Even when it doesn't look like our efforts are making a difference.

And Luther forgets this sometimes—that it's up to God, not to him.

Yes, sometimes he forgets. But he also often remembers it, especially in his writings, preaching, and hymns. There's a legend that when a student once asked Luther what he would do if he knew the world would end tomorrow, he said he would plant a tree today.

I love that! Precisely because the future is God's, and we can throw ourselves into caring for those around us—even and especially those who are different from us—today.

I like it too. Even if Luther didn't actually say it, it really captures his theology.

Which means the best way to deal with Luther's legacy—the good parts and the bad—is to trust God, to look for God to keep showing up where we don't expect God to be, and to act today because of the promise of God's love and life in the resurrection . . . no matter what.

Nicely put.

Now we're right back to where we began—with God's love for us and the world, and the freedom that creates at the center of things. This might be a nice place to stop.

Not stop, but pause. After all, we're still becoming what God has called us to be, and so we might rest, but then we'll look to see what God continues to do in us and through us for the sake of the world God loves so much.

I agree.

Or, as Luther might have said, "This is most certainly true. Amen."

Insights and Questions

Notes

Introduction

1. Ralph Waldo Emerson, *The Early Lectures of Ralph Waldo Emerson*, vol. 1: 1833–1836, ed. Stephen E. Whicher and Robert E. Spiller (Cambridge, MA: Belknap Press, 1959), 119.

2. *The Life Millennium: The 100 Most Important Events and People of the Past 1,000 Years*, ed. Robert Friedman (New York City: Bulfinch Press, 1998).

Chapter 1: The Reluctant Reformer

1. LW 45:70.

2. LW 32:112–113.

Chapter 2: Freedom!

1. Thomas Hobbes, *Leviathan* (1651).

2. LW 34:336–337.

3. Dietrich Bonhoeffer, *Life Together* (New York City: HarperOne, 2009), 91.

4. Gustaf Wingren, *Luther on Vocation*, trans. Carl C. Rasmussen (Eugene, OR: Wipf & Stock, 2004), 10.

Chapter 3: The Present-Tense God

1. Martin Luther King Jr., *The Strength to Love*, gift ed. (Minneapolis: Fortress Press, 2010), 47.

2. LW 39:188.

Chapter 4: The Ambidextrous God

1. LW 26:27.

2. LW 46:49–55.

3. James Madison, "To F. L. Schaeffer from Madison, December 3, 1821," *Letters and Other Writings of James Madison*, vol. III (Philadelphia: J. B. Lippincott & Co., 1865), 242–243, www.constitution.org/primarysources/madisonluther.html.

Chapter 5: Called for Good

1. Frederick Buechner, *Wishful Thinking: A Seeker's ABC*, rev. expanded ed. (New York City: HarperOne, 1993), 119.

2. LW 45:40.

3. LW 46:93–137.

4. LW 48:282.

Chapter 6: God Hidden and Revealed

1. LW 36:342.

Chapter 7: *Semper Simul*

1. Preamble, *Declaration of Independence*, 1776, www.archives.gov/founding-docs/declaration.

2. LW 31:53.

For Further Reading

Bainton, Roland H. *Here I Stand: A Life of Martin Luther*, reprint ed. Abingdon Press, 2013.

Bonhoeffer, Dietrich; ed. Victoria J. Barnett; trans. Barbara Green and Reinhard Krauss. *Discipleship. Dietrich Bonhoeffer Works: Reader's Edition*. Fortress Press, 2015.

Erwin, R. Guy, Mary Jane Haemig, Ken Sundet Jones, Martin J. Lohrmann, Derek R. Nelson, Kirsi I. Stjerna, Timothy J. Wengert, and Hans H. Wiersma. *By Heart: Conversations with Martin Luther's Small Catechism*. Augsburg Fortress, 2017.

Forde, Gerhard O. *On Being a Theologian of the Cross: Reflections on Luther's Heidelberg Disputation, 1518*, theology ed. Eerdmans, 1997.

———. *Where God Meets Man: Luther's Down-to-Earth Approach to the Gospel.* Augsburg Books, 1972.

Gritsch, Eric W. *Martin Luther's Anti-Semitism: Against His Better Judgment.* Eerdmans, 2012.

Herrmann, Erik H.; ed. Paul W. Robinson. *The Babylonian Captivity of the Church, 1520. The Annotated Luther Study Edition*. Fortress Press, 2016.

Hillerbrand, Hans J. *Christian Life in the World. The Annotated Luther, Volume 5.* Fortress Press, 2017.

King Jr., Martin Luther. *Strength to Love*, gift ed. Fortress Press, 2010.

Kittelson, James M., and Hans H. Wiersma. *Luther the Reformer: The Story of the Man and His Career*, 2nd ed. Fortress Press, 2016.

Kolb, Robert, and Charles P. Arand. *The Genius of Luther's Theology: A Wittenberg Way of Thinking for the Contemporary Church.* Baker Academic, 2008.

Marty, Martin E. *Martin Luther: A Life*, reprint ed. Penguin Books, 2008.

———. *October 31, 1517: Martin Luther and the Day That Changed the World.* Paraclete Press, 2016.

Oberman, Heiko A.; trans. Eileen Walliser-Schwarzbart. *Luther: Man Between God and the Devil*, reissue ed. Image, 1992.

Roper, Lyndal. *Martin Luther: Renegade and Prophet.* Random House, 2017.

Tranvik, Mark D. *Martin Luther and the Called Life.* Fortress Press, 2016.

Wengert, Timothy J. *The Freedom of a Christian, 1520. The Annotated Luther Study Edition.* Fortress Press, 2016.

———. *Martin Luther's Ninety-Five Theses: With Introduction, Commentary, and Study Guide.* Fortress Press, 2015.

———. *Reading the Bible with Martin Luther: An Introductory Guide.* Baker Academic, 2013.

———; ed. Mary Jane Haemig. *The Small Catechism, 1529. The Annotated Luther Study Edition.* Fortress Press, 2017.

———. *Treatise on Good Works, 1520. The Annotated Luther Study Edition.* Fortress Press, 2016.

Wingren, Gustav; trans. Carl C. Rasmussen. *Luther on Vocation*, reprint ed. Wipf & Stock, 2004.